The Wilderness Within

Meditation and Modern Life

Nicholas Buxton

CANTERBURY
PRESS
Norwich

© Nicholas Buxton 2014

First published in 2014 by the Canterbury Press Norwich
Editorial office
3rd Floor, Invicta House
108–114 Golden Lane
London EC1Y 0TG.

Canterbury Press is an imprint of Hymns Ancient & Modern Ltd
(a registered charity)
13A Hellesdon Park Road, Norwich,
Norfolk, NR6 5DR, UK
www.canterburypress.co.uk

Unless otherwise stated the Scripture quotations contained herein are
from The New Revised Standard Version of the Bible, Anglicized
Edition, copyright © 1989, 1995 by the Division of Christian Education
of the National Council of the Churches of Christ in the United States
of America, and are used by permission. All rights reserved.

British Library Cataloguing in Publication data

A catalogue record for this book is available
from the British Library

978-1-84825-657-6

Typeset by Manila Typesetting Company
Printed and bound in Great Britain by
CPI Group (UK) Ltd, Croydon

For all my teachers

Contents

Introduction

Wise Men from the East

It is often said that there is a great spiritual hunger in our society and there is plenty of evidence to suggest that this might indeed be the case. Residual belief in God, or some sort of 'higher power', remains strong – in spite of the best efforts of those who would see it eradicated – and although church attendance may be declining, a great profusion of 'alternative' spiritualities would seem to be flourishing. Consumerism may be the default 'religion' of contemporary life, but it clearly leaves many people wanting 'something more'. This is sometimes taken to imply that there is an inherently spiritual dimension to human existence, and that we all have spiritual needs, whether we choose to acknowledge them as such or not.

For all that, it just as often seems that the prevailing attitude towards spiritual matters is one of sheer indifference, rather than open-minded curiosity – never mind desperate hunger. Mainstream religion plays no part whatsoever in the lives of an increasing number of people, who appear to have little or no interest in spirituality of any description. Yet, even if we are not consciously seeking spiritual fulfilment, we are all seeking something. It could be love, pleasure, knowledge, power, success or transcendence: whatever we hope will satisfy the restless yearning that is the unmistakeable characteristic of human existence. This is why the notion of 'seeking something' indicates an implicitly spiritual thirst, albeit one that frequently comes packaged as yet another commodified lifestyle option.

These contrasting perceptions indicate that spirituality is a word with many meanings. Traditionally, it is the term used when talking about the experiential dimension of religious practice; hence Christian spirituality, Buddhist spirituality, monastic spirituality and so forth. These days, however, spirituality is more often defined independently of, or even in opposition to, religion. It is typically conceived in terms of personal values rather than institutional structures, as open rather than dogmatic, and humanistic rather than supernatural. Spirituality, as the term suggests, pertains to matters of the spirit, and the word 'spirit' – from the Latin for 'breath' – refers not only to the essence of life itself, but also those quintessentially human qualities that distinguish us from other creatures, such as our rationality, mind or consciousness. Spirituality therefore is about who and what we really are and, by implication, the values that shape us. It is often expressed as a quest for self-understanding and what it means to be human, which is why we associate spirituality with questions of ultimate concern. In fact, all these various uses are connected, since we can only really comprehend our identity in relation to that which transcends it.

The spiritual quest is, understandably, an important theme in the sacred literature of the world's great religious traditions. Examples in the Bible include the various migrations of the people of Israel, and the journey of the 'wise men from the East', who followed a star in the night sky that led them to the stable in Bethlehem where the baby Jesus was born.[1] Sometimes thought to have been Babylonian astrologers, the 'wise men' were clearly in the habit of reading the stars: not only for navigational purposes – as we still do to this day – but also for guidance of a more metaphysical kind. Indeed, the heavenly bodies – stars, planets, the sun and moon – were until relatively recently widely believed to have a direct influence over events on Earth. Astrology is a way of seeing human experience in terms of universal archetypes, which is why the stars were venerated as deities throughout the ancient world.

---

1 Matthew 2.1–12

Although we pride ourselves on being more sophisticated these days, nevertheless millions continue to consult their daily horoscope in newspapers, magazines and on the internet. We claim not to believe in astrology, yet we still ask people their star sign. Are we really any more 'rational' than those who lived in medieval or ancient times? I am not convinced that human beings have 'evolved' a great deal in this respect. We still obsessively follow the movements of the stars, and look to them for guidance in our lives, the only difference being that we have transferred the focus of our worship from the heavenly spheres to more earthly deities – actors, musicians, athletes and celebrities – the idols whom we revere and call 'stars'.

Just as our ancestors gazed in wonder at the stars in the night sky, so we look up to the stars of the entertainment industry and the contemporary archetypes they represent. We idolize them as the people who have it all: fame, fortune, good looks, a glamorous lifestyle and, above all, the ability to satisfy their every whim and fancy. We worship them; we want to be like them. And thanks to the advent of reality TV shows, promising a fast track to celebrity stardom, we too can live the dream. These days it is no longer necessary to have talent in order to be a 'star'. You can simply be famous for being famous. In fact, the celebrity industry has plumbed such depths of absurdity, and our appetite for vicarious stardom has become so insatiable, that now you can even be famous for not being famous.

Stars embody the collective dreams and aspirations of our culture and point us towards what we imagine really matters. They represent the guiding light that shows us the way to happiness. The wise men from the East were searching for something of ultimate meaning and value. And we too are searching for something: for love, fulfilment, satisfaction. We all are. It is simply a consequence of being human. Even when 'what really matters' is conceived in entirely self-indulgent or consumerist terms, it is still essentially what we hope will bring peace and contentment, the gratification of desire, and the end of our restless searching for 'something more'. Consumerism is the exploitation of this innate yearning, built on the erroneous belief that our happiness depends upon acquiring the wealth, possessions and brand identities that will enable us to live the dream of a better life. Advertising dupes us into thinking that something – preferably something endorsed by a star – is missing from our lives which, if only it were ours, would make us whole and complete. But we never attain that fulfilment because consumerism is not about the satisfaction of our desires but their constant stimulation; it is not about having things so much as perpetually wanting something else. And so we pour our energy into acquiring things we do not need, with money we do not have. But how can true and lasting contentment be the product of such vain hopes and fleeting pleasures?[2] Surely only that which is itself eternal can provide eternal joy? Surely only that which is ultimately real and true – that which some call God – can truly satisfy our restless, wandering souls? Seeking God – whether we would use that kind of language or not – is thus a basic function of being human. But how do we find God, the true God, as opposed to a mere idol of our own making? And what star should we follow to guide us on the right path?

The star that the wise men followed led them to the Christ child. And what did they find when it came to rest over the little town of Bethlehem? Certainly none of the razzmatazz of contemporary celebrity culture. There were no TV crews, paparazzi or fashionable socialites. Just a young mother and her baby, embodying the mystery of human existence, the mystery of God. So we have to ask ourselves: what star are we following? Or, to put it another way, what really matters? What do we really want, finally? For to know what you really want, the star you follow, the light in your life, is to know something about who you really are. This is the 'holy grail' of the spiritual quest. If we know who we really are, then it stands to reason that we will know something about the ground of our being, whether identified as the God in whose image we are made, or simply the deepest reality of what we are.

---

2 Ecclesiastes 5.10; Proverbs 27.24

We are spiritual nomads, wandering through the wilderness that is everyday life in the world: sometimes aimlessly, often lost, but ever seeking. We are all on a quest of one sort or another. For some, this might be understood as an explicitly spiritual search. For others, it might take the form of a hedonistic quest for the ultimate high. For most, it probably means just getting on with life and doing the best we can, trying to maximize happiness and minimize suffering. All our yearning – including our mundane desires and worldly aspirations – is essentially a manifestation of our longing for true and lasting fulfilment. Thus not only is the spiritual life a search, but the searching that characterizes life in general is implicitly spiritual. Yet, although spirituality involves searching for something, and may even be characterized as searching for God, there is an important sense in which it is not so much about seeking something as letting go of everything – especially the notion of being 'the seeker'. In other words, 'true' spirituality is not just another manifestation of consumerism, but quite the opposite.

The spiritual search is a search that ultimately leads nowhere, for its goal is simply the realization of who and what we truly and therefore already are. This realization only dawns when we let go of our attachment to everything we currently think we are. In the Bible, Jesus describes the Kingdom of Heaven – or the ultimate goal of the spiritual life – as being like a priceless pearl discovered by a merchant who immediately decides to sell everything he possesses in order to buy it.[3] That one pearl means more to him than everything else in the world put together. Unless we feel that the object of our quest is the most important thing in life, more important even than life itself, our effort is likely to be in vain. The spiritual life entails more than merely trying to fill the existential void caused by our insatiable desire for satisfaction. The spiritual life is life in all its fullness, the life that is truly life.[4] And at the same time, it is the life that is gained by letting go of life.[5]

---

3 Matthew 13.45–6
4 John 10.10; 1 Timothy 6.19
5 Matthew 10.39, 16.25; Mark 8.35; Luke 9.24, 17.33; John 12.25

This book is about life in general and the spiritual life in particular, though I hope you will soon come to realize that there is no real difference between the two. More specifically, it is a book about meditation – what it is, why it is important and how it relates to the rest of life – for meditation is the means by which we reach towards that deeper understanding of the way things are that we might call the knowledge of God. Although written by someone who is an 'official' representative of a mainstream religion – a parish priest in the Church of England – the approach here does not assume the normativity of Christian belief or practice. It is my hope that much of what follows will be consistent with the insights of other traditions, and also appeal to those whose spiritual identity may feel less clearly defined. This is not to say that I endorse the increasingly popular notion that one can be spiritual but not religious. On the contrary, I believe it is impossible to separate one from the other without detriment to both. Indeed, by drawing on the literature of the Bible – not only because of its sacred status within Christianity, but because it is one of the principal foundations of Western culture – I hope to show that personal spirituality and mainstream religion can, and should, go hand in hand.

The Bible might seem an odd point of reference for a discussion about meditation. At first glance, it appears mainly to be concerned with the exterior forms of religious life, and the often very public intervention of God in human history. Compared with the extensive discourses on the contemplative life found in the texts of some Eastern traditions, such as the sayings of the Buddha or the Upanishads, the Bible contains relatively little in the way of explicit instruction on how to pray or meditate. This is surprising when one considers that the practice of contemplative spirituality lies at the very heart of the Christian life, albeit sometimes concealed from view. One reason for this may be that the primary emphasis in the life of the Church tends to be on the corporate and the external, leaving the interior and personal to be seen variously as either slightly suspect or else some sort of professional specialism for experts. But, of course, personal spirituality and corporate practice – faith and works – are deeply and necessarily interconnected. The Bible may not contain explicit instructions on how to meditate, but almost every page of it reinforces the fundamental truth that faith is primarily about a relationship with God.[6] It is a way of life, not just a set of opinions.

There is no single way to practise meditation. There is no definitively 'right' way. This book neither claims to promote the 'best' way, nor does it try to present all the options. It assumes just one basic method, which can be practised by almost anyone. In spite of all the mystique surrounding it, meditation is actually very simple. It can be learnt in a few minutes, though it will very likely take more than a lifetime to master. So, if all you want is to learn a basic technique, then you need read no further than this brief introduction.

First, settle into a position in which you feel you can remain reasonably still for as long as you intend to meditate – whether that be 20 minutes, half an hour, or longer – without needing to move unnecessarily. If possible, though it is not essential, try to sit with your back straight and unsupported, either on a chair or on the floor, in a posture that is relaxed and comfortable but also poised and attentive. You can have your eyes closed, or leave them open. Most people usually find it easier to concentrate with their eyes closed, but if you wish to keep your eyes open, just pick a spot somewhere in front of you and hold your gaze there.

Then just breathe in and breathe out. Breathe normally, neither fast nor slow. Try to keep your attention focused on your breathing. Be aware of the breath coming in and the breath going out. Feel it at the tip of your nose; notice the coolness of the air tickling your nostrils. Feel it in your abdomen as your chest rises and falls with each inhalation and exhalation.

Many people like to use a prayer word or mantra, which, together with the breath, helps to anchor the attention and keep the mind from wandering. I recommend choosing a word or phrase of two syllables, which can be easily coordinated

---

6 2 Timothy 3.16–17

with the breath, but there are other possibilities. It does not have to be a word or phrase that means anything. In fact, there are certain advantages to using a mantra that has no ostensible meaning – not least the fact that we are less likely to engage in discursive thought on account of it.

And just carry on breathing in and breathing out. Breathing in and breathing out. Keep your attention focused on the breath. Keep repeating the word. Keep breathing in and breathing out. As thoughts arise – which they will – do not try to suppress them, as this only generates more thoughts. Simply try not to get caught up in them: just watch them come and go, quietly observing as if from afar. Whenever you become aware that your mind has drifted away from the here and now, gently let that thought go, and bring your attention back to the breath. And breathe in and breathe out. That is all there is to it.

Well, maybe not quite all . . .

I

You Know Not the Hour

Modern life is far too busy. One of the great ironies of the present age is that the more gadgets we invent and acquire, the more dependent upon them we become. The more that technology enables us to save time and ease our workload, the more that workload seems to increase, and the more our time is consumed by it. Our lives are governed by the systems that were designed to make life easier, precisely because they allow us to do more and more in less and less time. We have, in short, become slaves to the very things meant to set us free: our ability to do anything, anywhere, anytime means we have to do everything, everywhere, all the time. We are more connected than ever, and yet at the same time it sometimes feels as if we are becoming more and more disconnected. This is perhaps epitomized by the increasingly common sight of groups of friends – or even couples – sitting together playing with their smartphones rather than talking to each other. Indeed, we are so dependent on mobile communications technology that it seems almost impossible to imagine how anyone was ever able to do anything as simple as arrange to meet up with someone before the advent of email, text messaging and social media.

Not only did we manage, however, but many of those old enough to remember that dim and distant pre-digital past look back and wistfully imagine that we actually had more freedom in those days. Admittedly, most of the clever devices we take for granted do save us time, and do perform with greater efficiency tasks that previously required more time and greater effort. Yet not only do we feel we have less time to do everything that needs to be done, but we also seem to waste vast amounts of time too, whether watching trashy television, distractedly surfing the internet, or voyeuristically browsing the online profiles of people with whom we may have only the most tenuous of connections.

We are so busy, it seems, that we never stop to ask ourselves the blindingly obvious question: what is the point of all this busyness, all this doing? We are so busy striving towards a future that may not even come about that we hardly notice the present as it slips by into oblivion.[1] We live our lives haunted by yesterday or yearning for tomorrow, barely noticing today and never for one moment thinking that, without any warning whatsoever, our safe little world could suddenly fall apart as a result of any number of unforeseeable circumstances.[2] We are so busy, and yet at the same time we are sleepwalking through life without ever really being awake to the reality of the present moment. Possessed by our possessions, consumed by our habits of consumption, we store up illusory treasure for our illusory selves, rather than being 'rich towards God'.[3]

The spiritual life is about freeing ourselves from the bondage of our conditioning, and waking up from the hypnotic daydream that we have come to believe is 'normal'. It is about waking up to who and what we really are, waking up to the reality of those around us, waking up to the deeper truth of things. The notion of 'waking up' is a common motif in much sacred literature. Arguably most explicit in Buddhism – after all the Buddha is literally the 'awakened one' – it is also given due emphasis in the Christian tradition. 'Keep awake,' warns Jesus sternly in the parable of the foolish bridesmaids, 'for you know neither the day nor the hour.'[4] And indeed we do not. Whatever else it might be taken to imply, the readiness that Jesus urges upon us in preparation for the coming of the

---

1 Matthew 6.27, 31–34
2 1 Thessalonians 5.3
3 Luke 12.21
4 Matthew 25.13; Cf. Matthew 24.36–42; Mark 13.23, 33, 35, 37; Luke 12.40, 21.36

Kingdom of God can surely be understood as a metaphor for spiritual awakening or enlightenment. The call to wakefulness is therefore a call to follow the spiritual path and to apply oneself to a spiritual discipline. A similar theme can also be found in the letters of St Paul – to the nascent Christian communities at Rome, Corinth, Ephesus and Thessalonica – in which he frequently addresses the pressing need for awakening, whether from the darkness of ignorance, or the slumber of sensuality and self-indulgence.[5] This wake-up call remains our constant companion in the spiritual life: waking up is what it is all about. And it is urgent, for 'the day of the Lord will come like a thief in the night'.[6] We know not the hour.

The spiritual life is all about 'waking up', but this can be approached in a very wide variety of different ways. A person's spirituality could work itself out in a life of selfless service to the poor and needy, or a campaign of justice for the oppressed and marginalized. It might involve the pursuit of theological study and philosophical reflection, or the devout expression of heartfelt piety. If genuine, it will undoubtedly be marked by the flowering of insight, wisdom and compassion, and will require – and engender – deep humility. But whatever outward form it takes, it will have at its heart a core discipline or practice. This may involve a practice of living more skilfully and intentionally, or a discipline of self-awareness and moral responsibility. For many people, that discipline is likely to include the practise of some sort of meditation or contemplative prayer.

Definitions

In common parlance, meditation refers to various disciplines of mental and spiritual cultivation, often derived from Eastern traditions such as Yoga and Buddhism. The actual word

---

5 Romans 13.11; 1 Corinthians 15.34; Ephesians 5.14; 1 Thessalonians 5.2–3, 6

6 1 Thessalonians 5.2; Cf. Matthew 24.43; Revelation 3.3, 16.15

'meditation' comes from the Latin *meditatio*, which refers to the act of thinking or pondering. Hence, in ordinary English, to meditate simply means 'to think deeply' about something. It is also sometimes suggested that the Latin verb *meditari*, to think or contemplate, is related to both *mederi*, to heal, and *metiri*, to measure, both of which provide us with fruitful ways of thinking about meditation. The former, which gives us words like medical and medicine, emphasizes the obvious connection between spiritual practice and healing. The latter, from which we get words for measuring, such as meter and metric, as well as 'mete' – as in mete out judgement – suggests that spirituality is to do with putting things into perspective and seeing things as they really are. Thus, thinking about meditation in terms of healing indicates that it is about restoring balance and wholeness in our lives, while the notion of measuring reminds us of how we talk about getting the measure of something to mean coming to an understanding of it.

Indeed, it is interesting to note the extent to which, in one way or another, measuring pervades virtually every aspect of our existence. We are constantly asking how much, how long, how far or how many. Life is all about measurement and balance, which in turn is all about understanding and defining the relationship between things. This is no less true of the spiritual life, which has as one of its primary objectives the achievement of greater harmony in relationships – to others, to the world, and to God – once again implying both healing and measuring. Meditation, or the cultivation of self-awareness, is about seeing things as they really are and having a healthy, balanced perspective on life. It is no coincidence that many of the healing miracles attributed to Jesus in the Gospels involve restoring sight to the blind, as well as enabling the deaf to hear, the lame to walk, and so on.[7] Whatever may or may not have really happened, the analogy should be obvious.

---

7 Matthew 9.29, 11.5, 12.22, 15.30, 20.34, 21.14; Mark 8.25, 10.52; Luke 4.18, 7.21, 18.43; John 9.7

In the Christian tradition, the word meditation is sometimes used to denote a type of prayer. This can at first seem a little confusing. Prayer is usually thought of in terms of a verbal entreaty, addressed to God, in which we express our concerns, cry for help, or offer thanks and praise. It is most commonly done with a specific intention in mind, for or on behalf of someone or a particular situation. Meditation, on the other hand, is generally understood by most people to be something rather different, and which usually entails being silent. In Christian spirituality, however, prayer may be classified as either vocal or mental, though we should be wary of applying this distinction too rigidly since both work in a similar way. The former includes petitionary and intercessory prayer – whereby we pray with words, either for ourselves or others – while the category of mental prayer can be sub-divided into meditation and contemplation. In this context, meditation usually refers to a process of thinking deeply about something – such as a passage of scripture – in order to penetrate to its inner meaning, while contemplation, or contemplative prayer, is used to describe a wordless state of spiritual awareness or communion with the divine. Thus, contemplation is arguably the term that most accurately corresponds to the popular understanding of meditation, which – strictly speaking – has a rather more specific and slightly different application in the Christian tradition.

However, the widespread use of the term meditation to refer to various kinds of spiritual exercises, and the general acceptance of the word among Christians to denote the practice of contemplative prayer, has resulted in meditation and contemplation being used more or less synonymously. This book will use the word in its popular, everyday sense – rather than its precise theological sense – although meditation on scripture will feature prominently in our discussion of contemplative spirituality. My own definition is that meditation is a spiritual discipline, in which methods of training the attention and stilling the mind are practised in order to develop refined states of consciousness. This, in turn, should foster the cultivation of self-awareness, lead to a deeper understanding concerning what is ultimately real and true, and bear fruit as the humility, wisdom, compassion and skilful living referred to in the Bible as 'godliness'.[8]

Motivation

If the terminology is confusing, the hurly-burly of the spiritual marketplace is likely to be completely baffling. There is quite a demand for meditation these days, and this demand is being met by a multitude of extremely diverse providers. These vary from self-certified individuals to mainstream religious institutions, who between them offer a bewildering array of different teachings, techniques and therapies, with an equally bewildering array of reasons for why we should subscribe to their particular brand, method or programme. The explanations that people give for why they meditate, or why they think other people should meditate, cover everything from the treatment of physical ailments to union with the divine.

The following list, though by no means comprehensive, gives an indication of the range of values and benefits ascribed to meditation by some of its many practitioners. For example, meditation is practised in order to relax and unwind after a stressful day, or to calm the mind, alleviate anxiety and increase general health and well-being. It may be used to soothe pain – both mental and physical – to lower blood pressure, cholesterol and the risk of heart disease, as well as to treat phobias, addictions, insomnia and fatigue. Some claim it can reduce or even reverse biological ageing. Many see meditation as a tool to enhance mental clarity, concentration or memory, or to gain greater self-confidence and control over one's destiny. Thus meditation is employed as a technique for developing willpower or intelligence, becoming more focused, achieving desires, improving learning skills, creativity and sporting prowess, or being more productive in the workplace. For some people it is about

---

8 I Timothy 4.7, 6.11; 2 Peter 1.3; Cf. 5.22–23

acquiring inner peace, gaining a more balanced outlook on life, seeing the bigger picture, or cultivating compassion and being more connected with the whole of humanity. There are those who believe that by meditating they are helping to bring about world peace, while others may be seeking esoteric wisdom, spiritual insight or enlightenment. It is often understood as a way to acquire deeper knowledge of the inner self, the fundamental reality behind surface appearances, or to become one with God.

Given this rich profusion of different purposes, it is not surprising that there should be such an abundance of different schools, traditions, methods and techniques. The beginner could feel overwhelmed, or even put off, by the maze of choices on offer. Should they go for insight or mindfulness meditation, mantra chanting or shamanic visualization, new age or traditional? Not to mention Christian meditation, chakra meditation, Zen meditation, countless varieties of yoga, and a plethora of well-known 'brands' such as TM, Vipassana and so on. The list is endless: no wonder people who want to learn about meditation very often do not know where to start. Which path should they follow? What is the best way, or the right way? Whether we have some experience of meditation already – having attended a few classes, or read some books about it – or no experience at all, we may well feel swamped by the glut of available options, and thoroughly perplexed by all the mystifying jargon. The truth is, however, that the choice of method is one of the least important considerations. It is much more important that we understand our motivations. This is why, when people ask me to teach them how to meditate, I always start by asking them what they think meditation is all about – and, more importantly, why they think they want to do it – before getting on to the practical business of how.

There is likely to be a significant difference between meditating in order to cope with stress, and meditating in order to experience God. The purpose for which we meditate will determine not only what we think we are doing, and how we go about doing it, but also the 'results' we are likely to obtain.

It will colour everything. Not that there is necessarily a 'right' reason for wanting to meditate: in any case, our reasons will change over time. The point is that if meditation is about the cultivation of self-awareness, then surely one of the things we ought to be aware of is our reason for wanting to meditate in the first place. To put it another way, what is the 'problem' to which we imagine meditation might be the solution? Is it about coping with stress? Are we trying to address some personal issues? Or is there a bigger picture? Understanding our motivations in life is essential to understanding who we really are. But it requires a great deal of honesty and careful self-examination. Motivations can be complex, and we are very good at deceiving ourselves.

Not only do we need to become aware of our motivations, which may be deeply hidden, but we also need to try to become aware of what else our motivations may themselves be concealing. Discovering what lies behind them is no easy task and we should never be satisfied with the first answer we come up with, but rather dig deeper and deeper, sifting through the layers of our drives and desires. There are no right or wrong answers. And none of them will be the last word anyway. What is more important is that we keep asking the questions. If we do, we may find ourselves embarking on an unexpectedly revealing journey of self-discovery.

As we have seen, the reasons people give for wanting to meditate can vary enormously, but there are two main categories of motivation that predominate: relaxation and enlightenment. Together these form a spectrum that has the attainment of peace at one end and the acquisition of power at the other. Indeed, it is interesting to note how frequently the words 'peace' and 'power' appear in the titles of books on spirituality. Notions of peace and/or power permeate the ways in which meditation is taught, described and written about. You may notice it too in the way people talk or think about meditation, disclosing either their desire to find inner peace in order to counterbalance the stress in their lives, or a thinly disguised quest for some kind of power, whether envisaged in terms of personal charisma, enhanced mental abilities, esoteric knowledge or material success. Different people clearly use meditation in pursuit of different goals, and there will be a range of views regarding the merit or validity of these various aims. Both peace and power imply questionable motivations for spiritual practice, however, because both conceive of spirituality as a means to an end rather than as an end in itself.

When understood in terms of the attainment of peace, meditation is associated with the kind of spirituality that is often promoted as an antidote to the pressures of modern life. Spirituality reduced to little more than an exotic form of relaxation therapy will no doubt 'work', but to practise meditation solely in order to gain peace of mind is a far cry from the radical transformation, of oneself and the world, advocated by most spiritual traditions. There are plenty of ways we can relax, if need be, such as by going for a walk or listening to music; but while these activities may be a valued component of a spiritual practice, they are not the same as meditation. Meditation is not just about relaxation or making ourselves feel good. It is more intentional than that. Paul suggests as much when, in his letter to the Romans, he says, 'do not be conformed to this world, but be transformed by the renewal of your mind'.[9] Peace of mind is important, and not to be dismissed as a triviality, but true peace involves more than just the reduction of stress. True peace is the profound harmony with the self and the world, the deep personal integration that is, paradoxically, the consequence of a certain kind of detachment from 'the world'. And that takes some doing.

At the other end of the spectrum we find those who want to meditate in order to seek God or attain enlightenment. At first we might think this represents the 'right' reason for practising meditation. But again, it rather depends on what we think seeking enlightenment – or, for that matter, the knowledge of God – is all about. We may discover, for example, that this goal is often understood in terms of acquiring esoteric

9 Romans 12.2

knowledge and the power that we may imagine comes with it. Spiritual power is highly seductive and those who seem to have it can exert a huge influence on others. People look up to them, and invest them with their respect and love, increasing their authority still further. But, in common with any other kind of power, it encourages delusions of self-importance and the erroneous feeling of being somehow in control of things. An approach to spirituality that sees it primarily in terms of a personal achievement – however 'godly' it may be – serves only to feed our vanity and become another ego-trip. This is precisely the corrupting attitude that Paul denounces in his first letter to Timothy, where he describes false teachers as 'conceited, understanding nothing . . . imagining that godliness is a means of gain'.[10]

The problem in all of this lies not so much with peace or power themselves, but rather our tendency to think in terms of objectives to be attained, which only reinforces the egocentric illusion that we are the beneficiaries or 'owners' of the fruits of our practice. If you meditate in order to achieve such goals you may well be 'successful', but you will have missed the mark. Meditation is not really about anything that can be achieved, or a result to be gained. Peace and/or power, in one form or another, may indeed accrue to the practitioner of meditation, but whilst these might be among the consequences of meditation, they cannot be the purpose of it. Not that there is anything wrong with wanting to improve one's mental and emotional quality of life; the point is that focusing too closely on the detail may cause us to lose sight of the whole. Whether one is motivated by peace or power, the issue is much the same: such motivations are fundamentally egotistical, whereas the purpose of a spiritual practice is to give up living in thrall to the demands of the self and learn instead to live for something other and greater than the self, which ultimately implies that which we call God.

---

10 1 Timothy 6.4–5

A truly engaged spirituality surely cannot be reduced to a self-indulgent preoccupation with relaxation, or an egotistical quest for enlightenment. Meditation holds out the promise of a radical personal transformation that is considerably more worthwhile than striving for peace or power. Meditation is not about achieving goals, and still less about having 'spiritual experiences', which in any case would generally be considered a distracting and deceptive product of our own emotions. Indeed, the more extraordinary the experience or gift, the more difficult it becomes to maintain critical detachment and avoid being possessed by vanity and pride. The spiritual life is not to be confused with the 'experiences' that may – or more likely may not – accompany it. It is about simply abiding in the deepest reality of what we are. Far from being a matter of attaining experiences, it is, as a Buddhist monk once told me, about nothing more nor less than 'just trying to be normal'.

The practice of meditation involves being present to who and what and where and how we really are. This should lead to a revolutionary conversion of life, but only if we are able to give up our self-centred preoccupations with the acquisition of peace and power. The purpose of a spiritual discipline, or the cultivation of self-awareness, is to learn to see things the way they are, to act accordingly, and be transformed as a result. This is why wholeness and healing, or measuring and understanding, might provide a more suitable framework than peace and power when thinking about meditation. After all, the cultivation of self-awareness is not so much about personal fulfilment as the fullness of being human. True 'self-improvement' is not really about improvement of the self for its own sake, but in order to make the world around us a better place for others.

The importance of self-awareness, especially regarding our motivations, can be most clearly understood by seeing how the lack of it is so often a factor in so many of the innumerable 'issues' that afflict us in life, and which in turn drive us to seek peace and power in the mistaken belief that this will solve our problem. Lack of self-awareness can be seen in the common tendency to project onto others the faults of which we ourselves are most guilty. It can be identified as the root cause of personal conflict, it lurks behind all that obstructs us in the spiritual life, and it prevents us from being authentic. Indeed, it is nothing less than the fundamental ignorance, or 'not seeing', of which the Buddha spoke, and thus the cause of *Duhkha*, the word he used to describe the inherent unsatisfactoriness and frustration that characterizes the human condition. Similarly, in the Christian context, lack of self-awareness is implicated in the 'original sin' that leads to The Fall, and all the suffering that inevitably follows as a consequence.

According to the story in the Book of Genesis, before The Fall, Adam and Eve are in perfect harmony with God. They then eat the fruit of the tree of the knowledge of good and evil – symbolizing our tendency to make false distinctions and value judgements on the basis of comparing one thing with another – and the blissful oneness of self-awareness is replaced by the dualistic relativism of self-consciousness. Self-consciousness is the opposite of self-awareness. Self-consciousness places a thought of the self – together with an ego-based value judgement – in the way of the pure awareness of God, or reality as it is in itself. Paradoxically, the return to Eden, or the summit of self-awareness, is attained when all awareness of self disappears. But we still have to know ourselves in an ordinary, everyday way first. We have to know the imaginary, constructed self that we are not, in order to discover the true self that is the image of God within us. Eventually, we have to let go of the notion of self altogether, for as we come to know God the self disappears, like a shadow chased away by the light. To some, this may not sound like an appealing prospect. For others, it is the good news they have been waiting their whole lives to hear.

Technique

In spite of the fact that it is so important to be aware of our motivations – whatever they may be – most people seem to be more concerned with matters of technique. They are, in short, worried about method, and often appear to have much less interest in what they are doing and why. 'If only I can learn how to perform a certain technique absolutely perfectly', goes this line of reasoning, 'then I will achieve my goal.' Many thus see meditation as a kind of 'spiritual technology', which – if correctly mastered – will automatically result in the attainment of inner peace, self-knowledge and a calm, stress-free life, together with increased energy, concentration and productivity. Some teachers make a point of encouraging these inclinations – usually to their financial advantage – even promising that their particular brand of spiritual exercise will lead to the satisfaction of our material desires and aspirations as well. Those who think of meditation in terms of either peace and relaxation, or personal fulfilment and power, are often only really interested in what appears to be the 'best' technique; namely, the one that most persuasively guarantees the desired outcome.

None of this is to say that technique is not important. But just as 'success' should not be the primary motivation, neither should technique be the primary concern. In one sense, the right technique is whatever works for us. Any skill we may cultivate in our practice is simply a way of allowing something to happen – something over which we have little or no control – in the same way that opening a window does not actually cause the refreshing breeze to blow in, it just allows it. Paul expresses a similar idea in his first letter to the Corinthians, when he says, 'neither the one who plants nor the one who waters is anything, but only God who gives the growth'.[11] Of course it is true that we do have to do something. We have to open the window; we have to water the garden. But at the same time we also have to do nothing and remain still, because if we are too busy rushing about, we will never feel the cool breeze coming through the open window. Meditation is less about technique than attitude: an attitude of openness and humility. After all, the point of our practice is not simply to become good at meditation, but to wake up.

---

11 1 Corinthians 3.7

An obsessive preoccupation with questions of technique can be as much of a distraction as constantly striving to achieve results. Indeed both tendencies are closely related. But what matters more than either technique or results is having a proper understanding of how and why meditation – and prayer in general – actually work. To pray is to be 'still before the Lord, and wait patiently for him'.[12] Prayer – in both its vocal and mental forms – requires us to take a step back from ourselves, to put ourselves to one side, in order to be present to a reality that is other than ourselves. Prayer, in this sense, is nothing to do with asking for things, or trying to negotiate a deal – or, worse still, telling God what to do – although these are all common habits of the religiously inclined. Prayer is not a shopping list of all the things we want from God. Indeed, the notion of prayer as some sort of transaction is frequently condemned in the Bible. The prophet Amos castigates the Israelites for their spiritual materialism, and Jesus was well known for his sharp denunciation of the self-serving religiosity of the Scribes and the Pharisees.[13] When he instructs his disciples in prayer, he warns them not to be like the hypocrites, who make ostentatious public displays of their piety, 'for they love to stand and pray in the synagogues and at the street corners, so that they may be seen by others. Truly I tell you, they have received their reward.'[14] Instead, he exhorts them not to 'heap up empty phrases . . . for your Father knows what you need before you ask him'.[15]

Prayer is not – and cannot be – something we do for the sake of the results and benefits that will accrue to us, great though they may be. It is, rather, something we do simply for its own sake, as an end in itself. We pray, not because God needs our worship but because we need to offer it. In giving praise to God we express our capacity for love; the significance of this

---

12 Psalm 37.7
13 Amos 5.22–23; Matthew 15.7, 23.13–33
14 Matthew 6.5; Cf. Mark 12.40; Luke 20.47
15 Matthew 6.7–8

being that without love we are nothing.[16] Moreover, God does
not 'answer' our prayers by manipulating the circumstances of
life to our personal advantage, but rather by abiding in God,
by conforming to the will of God, we align ourselves with the
way things are – or should be – and thus become more adept
at playing the game of life ourselves. To be in harmony with
'what is' or, to put it another way, to be obedient to the will
of God, transforms our self-centredness into God-centredness.
In prayer we offer ourselves – all that we have and all that we
are – to God, in order, as the meaning of the word sacrifice
suggests, to make ourselves holy, as he is holy.[17] Prayer is the
means by which we become 'pure and blameless'.[18]

Of course, prayer can and should be about giving voice to
our concerns and intentions, and it is important that we do
this, especially in corporate acts of public worship such as
those that take place in church. But prayer is about so much
more than what we say. By expressing compassion for others,
and thus learning to transcend our own egocentrism, prayer
puts us into a right relationship with God, or that which is
ultimately real and true. Prayer is grounded in a humility that
acknowledges a reality other than the self. It is what enables
us to see the difference between the reality that is God, and
the unreal gods of our own making, thus preventing the self
from usurping the place of God and descending into idolatry.
Prayer requires us to take a step back from ourselves – even if
only for a moment – in order to see things in perspective and
as they really are. By the discipline of putting ourselves to one
side, and articulating our concerns for those in need, we take
the ego out of our relationship with God and our dealings with
each other, and learn to act more selflessly and thoughtfully.
This impacts on all whom we meet and affects all that we do.
Through prayer we not only make ourselves better persons, but
we also enrich the lives of those around us and contribute to

---

16 1 Corinthians 13.2
17 Leviticus 11.44; Cf. 1 Peter 1.13–16
18 Philippians 1.10

the sum of human flourishing by making the world – made up
as it is of people just like us – a better place. Prayer, or meditation, is often seen as a personal practice, but it is not private.
Prayer transforms individuals and through them the communities of which they are a part. To cultivate self-awareness is to
learn to see ourselves as others see us, and to see others as ourselves. A spiritual practice is not about personal achievements,
such as acquiring peace and power, but being true to who and
what we really are – that is, each other – and abiding in that in
which 'we live and move and have our being'.[19] Ultimately it is
simply to be.

In spite of the impression one may get that meditation is
all about technique – and a bewildering array of techniques at
that – the truth is there is actually nothing much to do when it
comes to meditation. It is more about an attitude. So we should
not think of meditation in terms of what we can gain from it,
or what it can do for us, but rather as something we need to
do – and keep doing – in order to sustain ourselves spiritually.
Our spiritual discipline should be seen as a form of essential
nourishment. It is no accident that the Lord's Prayer contains
the line 'give us this day our daily bread'. Bread here is not
just one of the various different things we eat: it represents our
staple diet, a basic necessity of life. The Lord's Prayer acknowledges that we depend upon God for our very existence, in all
sorts of ways, because God is the animating spirit of life itself.
In John's Gospel, Jesus is described as the living bread, that
which nourishes and sustains us: whoever eats this bread, he
says, will have eternal life.[20] This serves as a good metaphor
for meditation in other ways too. As we eat, food is assimilated
into our bodies; our bodies are literally formed out of what we
eat. The analogy holds for whatever we consume. Therefore,
as we partake of spiritual food, it will form us spiritually. Thus
the life of prayer, and participation in the worshipping life of
a faith community, changes us, forming us into the likeness of

19 Acts 17.28
20 John 6.35–40

the divine – which for Christians is represented by the person of Christ.[21]

It is worth remembering, however, that our physical hunger can never be truly satisfied. No sooner have we eaten and digested our food than we are hungry again. This is true of all our desires: as soon as we get what we think we want, we crave something else. Desire is unquenchable. The same also applies to spiritual hunger, in the sense that nothing of this world can ever really satisfy it, for our spirit hungers with an infinite yearning for the infinite itself. Only God, who is infinite and eternal, can satisfy the longing that can never be satisfied. All our desires – even those directed towards 'worldly' ends – are sublimated expressions of this fundamental desire for God, because all desire hankers after the ultimate satisfaction that will finally quench it. The eternal life that Jesus offers is nothing less than the reality and truth we call God. If this is what we truly desire then the first step on our journey must be to let God into our lives.

The metaphor of a journey in relation to the spiritual life may be a cliché, but like all clichés it contains an element of truth. The spiritual life is concerned with transformation, and a journey – any journey – necessarily entails change. This is true in an obvious sense: we undergo a change of location as we journey from one place to another. But there could also be deeper changes too, for we may be a different person on arrival from the one we were when we set out. It is apt, therefore, to characterize the spiritual life as a journey – we often talk about our journey of faith – because in fact all journeys require an act of faith. Faith that our expectations will be fulfilled. Faith in our ability to make it. Faith that the destination is one for which it is worth undertaking the journey in the first place. The Bible contains numerous accounts of epic journeys, such as that of the Magi who followed a star to Bethlehem, and Abraham who obediently answered God's call to set out for the Promised Land, 'not knowing where he was going'.[22]

---

21 John 14.7, 9; Cf. Colossians 1.15
22 Hebrews 11.8; Cf. Genesis 12.1

But perhaps the ultimate archetype of the spiritual journey is reflected in the wanderings of the people of Israel as told in the Book of Exodus.

The Israelites had to have faith in order to undertake their long and arduous journey, from slavery in Egypt to the Promised Land: a land they had not seen, but had to believe in, to take on faith. They had to have faith in Moses, that he would guide them safely. But before any of that, they had to be persuaded of the need for making the journey in the first place. They had to wake up to the reality of their bondage; they had to reach a point of crisis. And so do we. It is to a consideration of this initial and sometimes violent awakening that we will turn in the next chapter.

2

A Chasing After Wind

They say death and taxes are the only things of which we can be sure in this life. Well, taxes can be evaded – sometimes even avoided – but death? I think not. Death is non-negotiable.[1] It is the fixed horizon to which any account of human existence must always be tethered. Death is both that which gives meaning and value to life, and that which can sometimes make it seem as if everything we do and strive for is ultimately meaningless and futile. Whatever we may choose to believe to the contrary, there is no 'big picture' in which it makes sense – or at least, not one of which we can have certain knowledge. Regardless of what we think may or may not happen next, death is undoubtedly the end of everything we know and are at present.[2] 'When their breath departs', says the Psalmist, 'they return to the earth; on that very day their plans perish.'[3] Unless we are among the relatively few who have stared certain death in the face and somehow miraculously survived to live another day and tell the tale, we will find it very hard to imagine being confronted by the end of everything we know. How could we? Our non-existence is quite simply impossible for our mortal minds to comprehend.

And yet the one thing in life – perhaps the only thing – of which we can be absolutely sure, is that we are going to die.[4] Life is 100 percent fatal. But if I ask you whether you are

---

1 Psalm 89.48
2 Wisdom 2.1–5
3 Psalm 146.4
4 Wisdom 7.6

ready to go – right here, right now – you will almost certainly say no. Why is that? Why are you not ready? The chances are that, faced with this question, most of us will answer in the negative. But why? We have all got to die sometime, so why not now? What difference will it make if it is today or tomorrow? What do you still need to do? Phone home to say one last goodbye? Finish some very important project you are working on? Have a successful career, raise a family, buy a new car, learn to play the piano, do the washing, feed the cat? And then what? Then will you be content and ready to leave it all behind, forever? Most people, most of the time – except in certain particular or exceptional circumstances – will, of course, say no. They do not want to die. Not today, not tomorrow, not ever in fact. We live our lives labouring under the vain delusion that we can make plans for the future. And while there is an obvious sense in which we can and do and must make plans for the future, in another sense it surely is all 'vanity and a chasing after wind', as succinctly stated by the author of the Book of Ecclesiastes.[5] We do not even know what will happen tomorrow, never mind in years to come.

We are but a breath of wind, our days 'like a passing shadow'.[6] Like the nomadic people of Israel journeying through the wilderness with their tents, we too are in transit through life, a fleeting presence in a temporary abode, 'a mist that appears for a little while and then vanishes'.[7] No sooner do we come into this world, than we depart it, with little to show for our time here.[8] Yet we live, for the most part, in stubborn denial of the profound impermanence of all existence. And there are good practical reasons why this should be so. Life would be quite impossible if we did not make at least some assumptions about the future. At the same time, however, our finitude is a fundamental fact of human experience that demands a response,

---

5 Ecclesiastes 1.14
6 Psalm 144.4
7 James 4.14
8 Wisdom 5.13

which is why the shock of seeing the fragile contingency of existence for the first time is often what precipitates the spiritual
quest. Not surprisingly, the Bible contains frequent reminders
of our mortality, such as the parable Jesus tells about a man
who puts all his energy into amassing wealth, only for God
to turn around and say, 'You fool! This very night your life
is being demanded of you. And the things you have prepared,
whose will they be?'[9] Obviously this is not to say we should do
nothing, or surrender to the kind of fatalism that says everything is pointless because it has all been pre-determined. It is
rather that we should be alert to the reality of the present, doing
all that we do for the sake of something more important than
our own interests, because ultimately nothing really belongs to
us – not even our own life.

Of course, we can and should prepare for the future that
we hope to see, even though we cannot know whether we will
still be around in order to enjoy it. The Bible warns that those
who 'trust in their wealth and boast of the abundance of their
riches' have succumbed to the delusion that they will live forever, forgetting that death is the great leveller, for the wise perish alongside the ignorant and foolish 'and leave their wealth to
others'.[10] We take comfort in our achievements, complacently
believing that we can 'relax, eat, drink, be merry'.[11] And yet, we
know not the hour. Given the stubborn inevitability of death,
we should ask ourselves, at the dawn of each new day – if not
every hour – whether we are ready to die, right here, right now?
And if the answer is no, as it almost certainly will be, then we
need to ask ourselves why not? What difference will it make if
I live a few moments more? What do I feel I still need to do, the
accomplishment of which will then allow me to say, 'ok, *now*
I'm ready'?

We may be surprised at the answer.

---

9 Luke 12.20; Cf. Jeremiah 17.11; Matthew 16.26; Proverbs 27.1;
James 4.14; Psalm 39.6; Job 27.17–22
10 Psalm 49.6–10; Cf. Ecclesiastes 2.18–21
11 Luke 12.19; Cf. Psalm 52.7

If our spiritual practice is about the cultivation of self-awareness, or simply waking up, then we may find ourselves most rudely awakened when we become aware of our mortality, and all the frustration, limitation and suffering which that implies. Yet, seen more positively, to be awake is to live every day as if it were the first, and might be the last, rather than – as we normally do – living in a past we regret and for a future that may never happen. There is an urgency about the spiritual life: now is the only time we can wake up; now is the only time we can encounter God. This urgency is made strikingly apparent when Jesus calls his disciples to leave their old life behind – to die to their former selves – in order to enter into a new life with God. When one says, 'I will follow you, Lord; but let me first say farewell to those at my home,' Jesus replies, 'No one who puts a hand to the plough and looks back is fit for the kingdom of God.'[12] To another, who asks if he may first bury his father, Jesus curtly responds, 'Let the dead bury their own dead.'[13] And on a number of occasions he tells his disciples that if they would have their life they must lose it.[14] We can be in no doubt that the call to the life that is truly life itself really is a matter of life and death.

As we contemplate the terminal boundary of this life, beyond which we cannot venture, we are forced back to those fundamental questions. What is the point of it all? What is the purpose of my life? Why am I living? What am I doing? Soon we will all be gone, and then what? What is the point of anything? These are questions to which it can be hard to give satisfactory or conclusive answers. Indeed, some might say there are no answers. After all, it is impossible to know that which lies beyond the possibility of all knowledge. So, on the whole, we tend not to think about it and instead just get on with life – our work life, family life, or social life – whatever it takes to do

12 Luke 9.61–2
13 Luke 9.60
14 Matthew 10.39, 16.25; Mark 8.35; Luke 9.24, 17.33; John 12.25

whatever needs to be done. Not that there is anything wrong with pursuing a career or raising a family – far from it. It is just that if we get too absorbed in the so-called 'cares of the world', we are likely to forget about all those unanswerable questions. Admittedly, we might think that is a good thing. If such questions are unanswerable, then surely there is no point wasting our time worrying about them. The only trouble is, these questions never really disappear completely. We may think we have left them by the wayside, but they linger on, below the surface, often without our even being aware of their continued influence over our lives. Evidence of their lurking presence can be detected in our lack of contentment, our frustrations and desires, for beneath the quest for fulfilment lies a search for meaning and purpose, even if it is not consciously acknowledged as such.

You may object. You may claim to have no interest in existential questions. You may be content to think that all is well as it is. Or you may have decided that there are no answers and that the point of life is just to enjoy it to the full.[15] But ask yourself if you are truly happy and completely satisfied with everything about your life as it is right now. The answer may be yes, in which case you are more fortunate than most. I know I would not be able to say as much myself because there are so many things I want to do, and that I would like to change about the circumstances of my life. Indeed, a little self-examination reveals that I am constantly fantasising about things being other than as they are. In my idle daydreams I imagine myself doing a different job, living in a different house, driving a different car, and so on. This highlights a discrepancy between who I am and who I think I want to be. And I very much doubt I am any different to anyone else in this respect. The precise details will vary between individuals but, one way or another, we are all striving to fulfil a perceived lack, trying to achieve something, trying to get somewhere, to be or become something other than who and what we are at present.

---

15 Wisdom 2.6–9

Why is that, I wonder?

One possible answer might be that the things we do, the desires we pursue and the goals for which we strive, mask an unacknowledged, barely conscious, denial of our inevitable mortality. Consumerism feeds on this latent anxiety, which is what makes it a 'religion' – albeit one that promises a salvation that cannot possibly be realised. And so we make plans for an imaginary future – naively assuming that there will be a tomorrow – even though that is the one thing we cannot take for granted. But then, what else could we do? How else could we play the game? The reason we do the things we do is because just about everything we do is given a purpose that is related to an as yet non-existent but hoped for future, and given a significance determined by its finitude. The show must go on, albeit under the delusion that tomorrow will come, even though in the larger perspective there really is no tomorrow. We go through our lives like sleepwalkers, never for one moment thinking that pretty soon it will all be over. After all, death is something that only ever happens to other people.

So what is that fundamental yearning underlying all our impulses? What are we really seeking, whether we hope to find it in the things of the world, or the eternal spiritual reality said to transcend it? What, to put it bluntly, do you really, really want? I would hazard a guess that what you want, and what I want, and what pretty much everyone wants, can essentially be reduced to more or less the same thing: happiness, satisfaction, and contentment – freedom from suffering, frustration and limitation – in short, fulfilment. Human beings are, as far as we know, unique among living creatures in that we are aware of our mortality and capable of reflection upon it. This provides the wellspring for all the stories we tell ourselves to explain the meaning and purpose of human existence, which in turn provide the means by which we learn to live with the questions that we cannot answer. One way of coping with the brute fact of our mortality is by having a belief worth dying for. This becomes the story that gives life the meaningfulness which death apparently denies.

Stories

We live our lives by, in and through stories: be they the big stories of life and death articulated by the world's religious traditions, the stories we read in novels or watch on television, or simply the content of our everyday social interactions. Just listen to any conversation – however mundane it might be – and you will find that it consists almost entirely of storytelling, both personal and general. Practically everything we say, hear and see is a story of one kind or another. We tell stories because reality can only make sense to us when filtered through a lens of some sort and structured as a narrative: that is simply how we process the infinite complexity of reality as it really is.

Storytelling is both what makes us human and how we articulate, signify and understand what it means – to us – to be human. Thus the world as we experience it is a world mediated by language, telling a story of who we are, why we are here and what we ought to do about it. Our story, whatever it may be, is our attempt to comprehend and express that which is ultimately incomprehensible and inexpressible: the irreducible fact of our being. And so we relate the story of our lives, our experience of being human, to a bigger, collective and 'given' story from which, and in relation to which, we derive or construct meaning for ourselves. We are myth-making creatures, who inhabit a world made meaningful to us by the story we tell about our experience of it. The quest for knowledge and understanding that drives the great endeavour of human culture, our arts and sciences, is a quest not so much to discover facts – though these are certainly useful – but meaning and value.

Everything we say and do is part of a story. We are constantly trading stories with one another. Much of the time we are unaware that this is what we are doing; that we are living in a story about life, rather than living life itself. In case you doubt this, next time you are with a group of people just take a step back from the conversation and observe the extent to which it consists of storytelling. Someone might be telling a story about something that happened to them recently. Someone else might be telling a story about what their children did at school. And another person might be telling a story about something they heard in the news. Notice also how we reconstruct the past in our stories, embellishing details for dramatic effect, subtly changing the order of events, or confidently relating the things we wish we had said as if we had actually said them. People tell all sorts of stories, all of the time. Most of our ordinary everyday communication consists of stories. Once you start to realize this, you will also notice it in the things you watch on television, and the snatches of conversation you overhear in the pub or sitting on a train. Life is full of stories. The world – our world – is literally constructed from them: a web of meaning spun from the yarn of stories. And so are we. Stories are present in the things we say and the events we recollect, of course, but they also feature in the plans we formulate – whether concerning the next meal or the next holiday – and the comments we make about life in general. Stories are woven into the fabric of the dreams we dream of a better, happier, perfect future. And they seep into our thoughts as we try to meditate.

Storytelling is everywhere. Stories provide the raw material for the tangled hallucination we call everyday life. And at the same time our stories create a surrogate reality, giving our existence the narrative we would prefer it to have. This becomes most apparent in relation to the ultimate story we tell ourselves in order to make life meaningful in response to the problem of mortality. If death makes life meaningless then we need a story that tells us otherwise, that gives us a part in a bigger story, one that goes on after us, that takes us beyond ourselves, that tells us who and what we *really* are. We need, in other words, a story that contradicts the facts. This is among the functions of those stories that constitute our belief system, whether that be a religious faith we have adopted, or simply the default worldview of the society in which we live. A belief is an attitude we choose to hold in spite of the facts, in order to transcend the limitation imposed by 'the facts'. It may not have anything to do with truth in the way in which we ordinarily understand it because a belief is an attitude chosen for the sake of an ulterior motive, namely a perceived benefit. It is believed to be 'true', not necessarily in a factual way, but because it is of value, or conducive to human flourishing, or morally worthy. Beliefs need not be 'true', as such, though they may help us to be true. We want to believe in life after death, for example, precisely because death is the end of everything we know. Our story may not necessarily be true in the most commonly understood sense of what it means to say something 'is true', but rather is meant to be a story that contradicts the facts.

Not only do we naturally and automatically tell stories that give us a meaningful account of things, that create the meaning of life, but also we quite naturally and automatically relate our personal, individual stories to the shared stories that comprise what we call 'culture'. Think about the manner in which we consume stories about the lives of public figures and celebrities. Think about how children play, entering imaginary worlds – albeit worlds created for them by the entertainment industry – to construct narratives of identity and meaning by mimicking characters and re-enacting scenes from their favourite stories, films, computer games or TV shows. Note also that the question of truth, in the normal everyday sense, is not remotely relevant here. Children slip easily into the imaginative world of their games, acting as if the fantasy scenario they have created is real and true, while at the same time knowing full well that it is not really true.

Children are not the only ones who create meaning for themselves in this way. After all, they do it not because they are children but because they are human. We can see the truth of this by considering the role of the imagination in pre-modern literature, especially that which retains characteristics of an oral tradition. One of the most notable features of oral literature, which often survives even after it has been recorded in writing, is the extensive use of rhyme, repetition and exaggeration. It is easy enough to understand the reason for the first two. In a pre-literate culture, rhyme and repetition make it much easier to commit stories to memory. When it comes to the use of exaggeration, however, the contemporary reader might be inclined to assume that the extravagant hyperbole of pre-modern storytelling is simply evidence of the ignorant credulity of the 'dark ages'. During the course of the modern era we have become conditioned to equate the written word with factual accuracy. If we see something in print, we believe it to have a certain authoritative status. And so, because we generally take the written word literally, we assume that anything and everything in writing should be judged by the same criteria, regardless of its original context or purpose. Thus, when we read something that stretches our credulity beyond the limits of reason, we simply assume it must be fictitious. But is it reasonable for us to suppose that medieval people were any more gullible than we are? How do we know they took literally stories that we would now be more likely to dismiss as fantasy? Besides, it is not as if we are immune to credulity: we still believe in all sorts of nonsense. Just consider the number of urban legends and conspiracy theories currently in circulation; not to mention the taken-for-granted assumptions – concerning rights, democracy, progress and the free market – that undergird the consensus worldview of modern Western society. Superstition, irrationality and 'blind faith' are neither things of the past nor the preserve of religious enthusiasts.

The purpose of exaggeration in pre-modern literature is two-fold. First, like rhyme and repetition, it makes it easier to remember a story if certain features of it stand out. Second, it is used for emphasis, in order to bring out the significance of a particular point. The moral or meaning of our narrative shapes not only our own behaviour, but also by extension the world in which we live, giving human existence the significance we believe it has. Stories gain their meaningfulness, not by reference to a fixed truth 'out there', but by reference to other stories, which taken together combine to form a network of coherence in relation to each other, an emergent truth that becomes more than the sum of its parts. This process is especially noticeable in the genre of Christian hagiography – life stories of the saints –

in which we see fantastic exploits recounted in the context of, and with reference to, the grand narrative of the scriptures. We should not automatically assume that these legends are – or were ever – meant to be taken literally. Such stories are not necessarily to be understood as factual accounts of the matter, but ways of situating the trajectory of personal experience within the shared narrative of a common culture.

Thus we make meaning for ourselves by relating the story of our life to the repository of shared stories that define us and our worldview. This is just something that human beings do. In a previous age, that stock of shared stories would largely have been derived from the Bible and Christian tradition. Today we are more likely to construct meaning for ourselves in relation to popular culture – an opiate as powerful as any religion – which is why the media serves up the mythical lives of the rich and famous for our consumption. These stories are not really about them, of course, but us. The point is that living by, through and in stories is something that is natural to human beings in general, and not merely those who profess a religious faith. It is not just something some people do because they are unable to tell the difference between reality and fiction, or because they are gullible or superstitious, but rather something that human beings do because they are human beings. It is how we make the world meaningful to us. Just think again for a moment about the way in which children play by instinctively entering into the imaginative world of stories, becoming their favourite characters, and acting out dramatic fantasy scenarios that bring their lives to life.

This could be one reason why Jesus says to his disciples – and therefore also to us – that unless you 'become like children, you will never enter the kingdom of heaven'.[16] In other words, unless we use our imagination – as children naturally do when they play – we will never see the world through the eyes of faith. It is important that we understand what this means. Living a life of faith is not primarily about giving our assent to a list

---

16 Matthew 18.3

of doctrinal propositions. Still less is it a matter of advancing factual claims that are at odds with everything else we know to be true about the world, and which only leads to cognitive dissonance and the proliferation of compensatory delusions. Rather it is to live life in a way that is meaningful, purposeful and imaginative. It is to live as if the story is true. This is what Christians do every time they gather for the Eucharist: the ritual representation of the shared story that determines their worldview and identity. Those who participate in that story commune with it; they even consume it – literally – thus defining themselves by it and making it part of the reality of their lives. By doing this they are taking the uniquely human capacity for inhabiting a story that makes sense of things to its logical conclusion. To make the world meaningful by means of telling a story about it is the essential function of religion. It is an entirely natural and instinctive human behaviour, the inevitable consequence of having self-awareness. And we all do it, all the time, whether we are religious or not.

Living in and through stories is not an optional choice: it is part of being human. But generally we are unaware of the fact that this is what we are doing. By practising meditation, however, we may learn to see our stories for what they are, and become more conscious of the ways in which we live our lives vicariously, in and through our stories. This in turn may lead to growth in self-awareness, and the possibility of freeing ourselves from some of the stories in which we may be trapped. We may even learn how to change our script.

Exodus

Very often people have their interest in spirituality awakened by the gnawing realization that something is not quite right in the world. It may be little more than a vague feeling that there should be more to life; it may be provoked by a major personal crisis. Essentially, we discover that there is a problem with our story. It needs re-writing. This is why answering the call to follow a spiritual path is likely to turn our world upside down. We will be forced to reassess everything we thought we knew, and all that we imagined was important. We will find ourselves travelling through unfamiliar territory to an unknown destination. And at times, we will wonder what we are doing and why we are doing it. This was certainly how the people of Israel felt as they trudged through the wilderness after their dramatic escape from slavery in Egypt. They doubted their leaders, they questioned their objectives, and they were often distracted from their purpose.

The Exodus story provides us with a sharply observed allegory of the spiritual journey, both in terms of the overall narrative sweep, and in many of its details too. Seen through this lens, the people of Israel – the children of God – represent the soul or 'higher self', while Pharaoh represents the ego or 'lower self', the 'passions' that dominate us. Pharaoh is the tyrannical ruler of the body, the enslaver, stubborn and difficult; Moses, the leader of the people of Israel, is our spiritual impulse or the 'higher self'. At first he feels inadequate to the task God calls him to undertake.[17] But once he submits to the will of God – or aligns himself with the way things are – he finds himself able to do things that previously he did not imagine himself capable of doing. God then sends Moses to entreat Pharaoh, in the name of the Lord, to 'Let my people go, so that they may worship me.'[18] This is the call to wake up and throw off the bonds of servitude and return to the Lord, or the true purpose of existence. But the Israelites, representing the individual soul, are enslaved; and their slavery is very much like our own. Like us, the Israelites are preoccupied with material concerns. Like us they are subject to anger and the blindness it causes – witness the two men fighting, and the fact that they reject the intervention of Moses. Like us, they care for little else but food and bodily comfort – as becomes apparent in the wilderness when they complain of the hardships and deprivation they have to

---

17 Exodus 3.11, 4.10–13
18 Exodus 8.1; 5.1; 7.16; 8.20; 9.1, 13; 10.3

endure on their journey. The slavery of the Israelites thus symbolizes the yoke under which we all suffer: as slaves to our conditioning, to desires that are not our own and to the illusions of choice foisted on us by the consumer society. Worst of all, we do not even realize that we are slaves. Like the Israelites, we need to wake up and throw off the chains that bind us to the things we have allowed to rule our lives, and seek instead what really matters, or that which is truly worthy of being called 'Lord'.

One of the most memorable episodes of the Exodus story concerns the ten plagues that God brings upon the Egyptians in order to punish Pharaoh for his stubbornness and to persuade him to let the Israelites go free. The plagues are thus indicators of God's power – or even just his existence – both for the Israelites, so that they may know that their God is God, and for the Egyptians, to teach them a lesson.[19] They are signs indicating that we need to turn away from self-centredness towards God-centredness; signs that show we are not in charge, that everything belongs to God, and that everything is God, 'whose spirit is in all things'.[20] As such they also serve as metaphors for the afflictions that may result from unskilful, or unspiritual, living. They are the psychosomatic symptoms of sin, the result of not seeing things the way they really are, and not acting accordingly. The behaviour of Pharaoh in response to the plagues reflects the behaviour of our own mind when it is dominated by the ego. Pharaoh is stubborn and proud. He fails to see the signs. And he is fickle, continually wavering, unable to stick to his decisions. He frequently changes his mind, agreeing to let the Israelites go and then refusing once more.[21] And we too, when confronted by the afflictions and obstacles of life, can become both stubborn and indecisive. Like Pharaoh, trapped in the spiritual darkness of his 'lower' self, we very often turn out to be our own worst enemies.

---

19 Exodus 9.16
20 Wisdom 12.1
21 Exodus 7.14; 8.8, 32; 9.7, 28; 11.10

Pharaoh is unrepentant. He will not turn from his arrogant, self-centred ways. He is stuck in the prison of his ego, unable to move on or grow spiritually. The first step on any spiritual path must be repentance, which is an immediate and natural response to the dawning awareness that something is wrong in the world and in our lives. It is no coincidence that in his mission to prepare the way of the Lord, John the Baptist focused on calling people to repentance, calling them back to the truth that is God.[22] And, indeed, Jesus also begins his public ministry with the same imperative.[23] Repentance – turning away from the self and turning towards God – is the necessary prelude to the spiritual journey. The realization that all is not as it should be, that there must be something more, is the wake-up call that prompts us to undertake a spiritual practice in the first place.

If we interrogate our constant search for satisfaction, whether of our physical desires, professional ambitions or personal goals, then we will have to admit that everything is not all right as it is. We would not feel the need to seek satisfaction if we already had it. If we continue to examine our pursuit of satisfaction, we may come to see that chasing after all the things we think we want will not bring us lasting contentment, but only further frustration and suffering. The pursuit of pleasure for its own sake does not bring pleasure, just as drinking to get drunk leads not to merriment but misery. All desire is ultimately idolatrous. Yet still we are driven – in everything we do – by something like an instinct to strive for whatever it is we imagine will result in perfect fulfilment. Thus our seemingly innate longing for 'something more' rests on the assumption that things – the world, life in general, oneself – are, or are experienced as being, somewhat less than ideal. We live in a 'fallen' world, a world that is imperfect and in which there is a great deal of pain and suffering. In addition to the obvious manifestations of physical suffering – such as violence, sickness and poverty – there is also what we might call existential suffering, which we experience as

22 Mark 1.4; Matthew 3.2, 8; Luke 3.3, 8
23 Mark 1.15; Matthew 4.17

the frustration of not getting what we want, being compelled to pursue desires that cannot be fulfilled, and the disappointment of never gaining true satisfaction. In short, all this 'unsatisfactoriness' comes about because we are out of sync with reality. Our illusions clash with the way things are, giving rise to what we might call the problem, whether real or imagined, of being human; the problem to which we believe a spiritual discipline might be the solution.

Therefore, whatever our reasons for engaging in a spiritual practice – even those criticized in the previous chapter – the implication is that we need to change something about ourselves or our experience of life. To put it another way, spirituality is about having compassion – that is, waking up to the reality of suffering in ourselves and others – and making a commitment to do something about it. Presumably we would not think we needed to practise a spiritual discipline if we did not think there was something wrong, or a question in need of an answer. We will only be ready to undertake the spiritual journey when we have had our fill of this all-pervasive unsatisfactoriness, when we are heartily fed up of it, and willing to banish our idols forever in favour of that which is ultimately real and true. This fundamental unsatisfactoriness, epitomized by the inescapable fact of our mortality, is the unconscious motivation underlying all that we do. Becoming aware of it presents us with the primary impulse to wake up. But this does not signal the end of our problems. In fact it may well be just the beginning of them.

The Israelites had to reach a point of crisis to force them to undertake their journey. Things had to get really bad. Becoming aware of the suffering and frustration of human existence – original sin or, in Buddhist terms, *Duhkha* – is the principal catalyst for entry into the spiritual life. The first followers of Jesus understood that we become 'partakers of the divine nature' when we 'escape from the corruption that is in the world because of lust' and answer the call to 'life and godliness'.[24] Paul describes how salvation depends on renouncing 'impiety and

---

24 2 Peter 1.3–7

worldly passions' in order to 'live lives that are self-controlled, upright and godly'.[25] Interestingly, both Christianity and Buddhism proffer the same diagnosis of the cause of our existential suffering: 'your cravings that are at war within you'.[26] It is only when we wake up to the fact of our bondage and become aware of the emptiness of our craving for all the things we think we want – the 'fleshpots of Egypt', as it were – that our journey can properly begin. We need to desire liberation above all else in order to make that effort to break free from our past and change our lives for good. The Psalms speak of the soul thirsting after God 'as a deer longs for flowing streams'.[27] If we are really serious about it, we will crave the life of the spirit more than someone who is drowning wants air.

So the question we need to ask ourselves is this: what do I really, really want, finally? What is that treasure so valuable that a man would sell everything he has in order to buy the field in which it is buried?[28] In other words, what *really* matters? We must keep asking ourselves this question if we wish truly to understand our desires and motivations. For example, we may think we are motivated by a noble wish to help someone in need, purely for their sake, but behind that there may also be an unacknowledged desire to feel good about ourselves for doing so. No value judgement is implied. It is just that we need to understand what is really going on, and where and when the ego is at work in the things we do, because it would seem that the truly disinterested action – with no personal expectations – is exceptionally rare. Even seemingly altruistic motivations may turn out upon closer examination to be driven by subtle forms of selfishness or desire for self-aggrandisement, personal gratification or recognition.[29] Jesus calls us to reject this kind of outward self-sacrifice in favour of true sacrifice

---

25 Titus 2.11–12
26 James 4.1; Cf. James 1.14–15; Ephesians 2.1–3; Galatians 6.8
27 Psalm 42.1
28 Matthew 13.44
29 Mark 12.41

of the self. But in order to do this, we need first to understand what we really, really want, finally.

The problem is that, generally speaking, we do not know what we really want, so a conflict arises within us, which inevitably overflows into our lives.[30] Paul knew this only too well. In his letter to the Romans, he reflects on the 'war' between the flesh and the spirit, lamenting the fact that he does not do the thing he wants, but the very thing he hates.[31] If we wish to resolve this dilemma, we will need to understand the difference between what we really want and what we think we want, which in turn is a question of working out why we are doing what we are doing, and what we hope to achieve by it. We have to be able to see what it is that is being fed when we act out of our stories and conditioning, and how the ego is reinforced by the things we do and the games we play – albeit sometimes unwittingly. And we need to discover what will instead bring us true peace and contentment, completely and finally. What is the satisfaction we seek in order to relieve ourselves of the restless agitation of our never satisfied desires, once and for all? What, in other words, really matters?

Try to explore this question, and see where that exploration takes you. What do you end up with? There may be many things you desire, many states you wish for, but will any of them bring you lasting fulfilment? Will whatever it is you think you want really bring permanent happiness, peace and satisfaction – completely, absolutely, finally? If we explore this question, we eventually end up with . . . with what? We cannot say. In the end, we may simply reach a wordless ultimate, beyond all the things we can enjoy and the satisfactions we can imagine. It is just 'what really matters'. And this is one of the things people are talking about when they talk about God. We end up with God, because nothing less will do.

---

30 James 4.1–3
31 Romans 7.15, 19; Cf. Matthew 26.41

3

Treasure in Heaven

Everyone has, at some point, wondered whether there is any kind of life beyond death. The question is rooted in a deep-seated anxiety about the meaning and purpose of human existence, as if at the very core of our being we cannot accept the inherent contradiction and profound meaninglessness that would be implied by 'non-being'. Our very essence revolts against it, and this reaction manifests as what we sometimes call the 'will to be', or the survival instinct: the basic drive behind everything we do, expressed in our lives as all the various forms of our innate desire for freedom. Freedom from the limitation of the ego, freedom from the limitation of mortality, freedom, even, from the desire for freedom itself. All the many desires we experience can be reduced to the desire to perpetuate our existence in some way, to exist in and for a future, and to transcend our inevitable and ultimate non-being. But even that most primordial instinct can be reduced still further, to a fundamental intuition that that which is, being itself, cannot not be. And the reason we know this is because that, in essence, is what we are.

No wonder we are in denial, living our lives as if there will be a tomorrow. After all, the notion that we will have an existence in the future is precisely what gives meaning to the present. We see this denial at work in our restless quest to find fulfilment, as we search for an ideal of happiness and fulfilment that always lies just over the horizon, where the grass is invariably a better shade of green and everything is just the way we want it to be. Then again, what other way could we live? Our instinctual – if unconscious – repudiation of our own mortality impels us to create meaningfulness in the face of meaninglessness. In other words, it is precisely because we are faced with the prospect of non-existence that we strive to understand, explain and justify the meaning of our existence in the meantime. Death has the potential to evacuate life of all meaning, and yet were it not for the inevitability of death, life really would be meaningless. If we were condemned to live forever, then nothing would have any value because an eternity of being would be indistinguishable from an eternity of non-being. So we create the meaning of our lives in the absence of a generalized 'Meaning of Life', and this enables us to endure and transcend the suffering, frustration and all-pervasive unsatisfactoriness that characterizes the human condition. Without a reason to live – or, to put it another way, a belief in something worth dying for – life would be unliveable. This is why human beings have, throughout the history of their existence, sought ways of comprehending their lives in terms of a story that somehow mitigates and makes sense of their fini-tude. That is, a story that contradicts the brute fact of life's fleet-ing transience, which on the one hand threatens to render life meaningless and pointless, and yet at the same time is the only guarantee of any kind of meaning and value at all.

What else could we do other than live life according to some sort of a story that more or less made sense? We may not know the purpose of human existence, but living in and through a story in which life transcends death, and meaning overcomes absurdity, enables us to believe that there is more to life than this, thus giving our existence a sense of meaning and purpose it might otherwise not have. This story of life and death and all the rest is what we might call the 'big story', our worldview or religion, the story that makes sense of what would otherwise be nonsense, the story that makes existence meaningful under the ever-present shadow of our ultimate non-existence. This is the story that frames our memories and articulates our hopes; that helps us resolve and integrate the disjunction between what we know and what we know we cannot know. And we need such a story, because we need to be able to tell ourselves that we have some idea of what it is all for; otherwise life just seems meaningless and absurd, and the universe becomes arbitrary and pointless, existing for no reason. And for some reason, we cannot accept that.

So instead we tell ourselves a story with a happy ending. There are different versions of this story. Some people talk of reincarnation, others of resurrection. A few believe that the story ends with this life; most believe that somehow life goes on, that death is relative rather than absolute. But what does it really mean to believe in life beyond the demise of the physical body? Often it seems to be taken for granted that the notion of life after death entails something like the person I am now continuing to exist – as me – after I die. Indeed, this is the assumption usually made both by those who believe in some idea of an afterlife and those who dismiss it. But is this really the right way to think about it? Given the emphasis on these matters in mainstream Christian belief, people are often surprised to learn that the Bible actually has very little to say on the subject of life after death, heaven, hell and all the rest. In the Old Testament, Sheol, the abode of the dead, is conceived as a realm of silence, of non-being; the word literally means pit or grave. In the Book of Job it says that 'those who go down to Sheol do not come up' and that we 'lie down and do not rise again'.[1] In the time of Jesus at least one Jewish sect, the Sadducees, explicitly denied the concept of a soul or life after death.[2] Having said that, it was clearly believed that God could bring the dead back to life again.[3] Indeed there are various accounts in both the Hebrew and the Christian scriptures of this happening. On the whole, however, it is generally accepted that popular beliefs about the immortality of the soul owe more to the influence of Greek philosophy than the Bible. It is from the Greek tradition that we get our enduring notions of mind–body dualism: the idea that the mind or soul – the two are often conflated – is an entity

---

1 Job 7.9, 14.12; Cf. Psalm 49.11; Wisdom 2.1
2 Matthew 22.23; Mark 12.18; Luke 20.27; Acts 23.8
3 1 Samuel 2.6; Psalm 30.3, 49.15, 86.13

that exists in its own right, independently of the physical body. This autonomous, self-existing and immortal soul, moreover, is taken to be our real self, the essence of our being, which somehow transcends the material realm and is thus able to survive the death of the 'merely' physical body.

Unfortunately, however, you need only do a little thinking around this area to realize that it can start to get awfully complicated. Which version of 'me', for example, do we suppose will survive our death? And in any case, how would it be possible for an immortal soul – identified somehow with our mental life – to have an autonomous existence, independent of the physical body? Surely the mind depends on embodied experiences for all its content. Without a body, and specifically its organs of sensation, not to mention the physical world with which it interacts, there would be nothing for the mind to think. It could not be. If that is so, then I – my soul, my true essential being – cannot simply be equated with my mind, memories, or some vague notion of 'consciousness'. An intrinsic part of who and what I am is the physical person whose empirical existence and particular characteristics can be apprehended and verified by the senses of another. Indeed, it is this tangible objectivity – rather than some nebulous, subjective 'essence' – that defines 'me', which is why it is often asserted that although dualism may be a common assumption, it does not really fit with the rest of Christian doctrine. The fact of the matter is that there has always been a consistently holistic strand in Christian thinking. After all, in Jesus Christ two natures – human and divine – are said to be one. To profess, as Christians do, belief in bodily resurrection would seem to imply that both body and soul together are necessary and essential components of the human person. Whatever the first witnesses to the resurrection may have experienced, it was neither a resuscitated corpse nor a ghostly apparition.

If the notion of life after death does not simplistically refer to the survival of a mental or spiritual identity that is somehow separate from the physical body, how then are we meant to understand it? Clearly there is no way of obtaining certain knowledge about life after death one way or the other. But perhaps there could be a different way of looking at it, a way of comprehending the idea of eternal life in terms of this life, because whatever else it might mean, 'eternal' cannot simply mean 'very long', as that would still be in time. The truly eternal must be outside or beyond time altogether. Eternity is timeless – it refers to that which is ultimately real, that which does not change or fade away – and the only time that is timeless is the present. Somehow, we need to understand 'eternal life' in relation to the here and now.

When a rich young man asked what he must do to inherit eternal life, Jesus bluntly replied, 'sell your possessions, and give the money to the poor, and you will have treasure in heaven; then come, follow me'.[4] And elsewhere he tells us that if you would have your life, you must lose it.[5] Jesus is not talking here about some notion of everlasting life after death, but real and authentic life here and now: a life that is not compromised or made meaningless by death, 'the life that really is life'.[6] If we wish to obtain what is real, we have to give up what is false – the ego and its empty projections – and instead invest our identity in what really matters and really is eternal: that treasure in heaven, 'where neither moth nor rust consumes'.[7] To talk about eternal life is to talk about our participation in the life of God, or that which is ultimately real and true: life in the presence of God, here and now. If eternal life is life lived present to God, who also somehow signifies the deepest reality of what we are, then in order to understand the notion of eternal life we need to be able to answer the fundamental existential question: who am I? What is the real essence of me? Any account of life beyond this life will first depend on understanding who or what really exists, here and now.

---

4 Matthew 19.21; Cf. Mark 10.21; Luke 18.22
5 Matthew 10.39, 16.25; Mark 8.35; Luke 9.24, 17.33; John 12.25
6 1 Timothy 6.19
7 Mathew 6.20; Cf. Galatians 6.8

Soul

People often talk a lot of nonsense when they talk about the soul, so we need to be clear. Briefly stated, the popular notion of the soul is the idea that there is some kind of immaterial entity or essence, whose existence does not ultimately depend on the physical body, which is somehow who and what we really are. To believe in the soul is to insist that there is a real 'me' that endures through all the changes of life – and beyond – and that this constitutes some sort of an 'owner' of all our various experiences of life in the world. But while we undoubtedly have the feeling of being a 'self', no such 'me' can be located or defined. When we look for this 'real' self, or soul, all we find are various naturally occurring and constantly changing experiential phenomena, none of which constitute a permanent, independent, self-existing self.

While belief in the idea of the soul is common currency in many worldviews, both religious and secular, any attempt to define or identify exactly what it is soon flounders. This has led some to reject the idea of a separate and permanent soul entity altogether, though this is not to say there is no self. Clearly we have a sense of self, and yet – in a view shared by hard-nosed neuro-scientists, trendy postmodern intellectuals and other-worldly Buddhist monks – there is nothing to which we can point and say 'that's it'; nothing that meets the definition of a soul entity. Indeed, all the things with which we identify as 'me' or 'mine', both material and mental, including our possessions, the place we call home, our personal appearance, interests, occupation, reputation, thoughts, memories and achievements, fail to meet the criteria of a 'real self' that is permanent, self-existing and so on. All of the above are variously used to create our identity – for the notion of owning something implies an 'owner' – yet none of them can be said to constitute the self. The self is thus revealed to be a psycho-social construct, a convenient label, but not any kind of 'thing' as such.

Contrary to the way in which we instinctively conceptualize ourselves as having an enduring essence, the self is not fixed but fluid, not autonomous but contingent, and not permanent but ever-changing. What we call our 'self', then, is a rut worn into the infinite, beginningless, endless stream of consciousness, a habit into which we slip, a vague idea that has taken on the appearance of solidity. It 'exists' – as a reflection of other selves, and all the various projections and attachments with which we identify as I, me and mine – but it is not what we think it is.

Indeed, because the self has no essential being as an entity in its own right, it can only exist by being seen to exist, which explains why we find the experience of feeling invisible to be so utterly soul-destroying: it is to feel as if we do not even exist. To put it another way, without regard we are nothing. Significantly, the word 'regard' has meanings that include both 'looking at', and 'holding in esteem'. Our self is thus made real by the regard of others – our very existence depends on being seen and valued – which is presumably why we so desperately crave attention, whether consciously or not. Observing the behaviour of babies and little children, one could argue that our most basic human need is not for food, shelter or some other expression of the survival instinct, but love, for it is love that guarantees our existence at the most profound metaphysical level. Once our basic physical needs are met, what we really want above all else is to be seen, to count for something, to have value, to be regarded, to be loved and affirmed. The feeling of being loved, or just held in some sort of regard, makes us feel like we matter. Ultimately it constitutes the very ground of our being: it really is true that to be seen is to exist. This is why we think of God as love. Love is our greatest need. To be loved is fundamentally necessary to our existence; without love we are nothing.[8] And so God becomes the projection of our need to be loved: love objectified and reified, the guarantor of our existence, creator of all that is.

It is odd, given all the assumptions we make about the soul – assumptions that are often taken to be core elements of Christian

---

8 1 Corinthians 13.2; Cf. 1 John 3.14, 4.8

doctrine – that in fact there are few statements concerning the soul to be found anywhere in the Bible. The word is used often enough, but it is never explicitly defined or explained. However, we can find one or two suggestive hints if we look carefully. In his letter to the Galatians, for example, Paul says that in Christ we are all one. 'There is no longer Jew or Greek, there is no longer slave or free, there is no longer male and female; for you are all one in Christ Jesus.'[9] But what did he really mean by that? This controversial remark was made in the context of a discussion about the status of Gentile converts and whether or not Christians needed to observe the Jewish law. On the face of it, Paul is saying there is an equality among those who share the faith of Christ that transcends worldly distinctions.

But these words also say something about the difference between the true self and the false self; who we really are and who we think we are. Note that the three categories Paul mentions – ethnicity, class and gender – are all social identities that are generally regarded as constructs: that is, not really real. Being a Jew or a Greek – not to mention British, for that matter – is an accident of birth. To say that I am British is true at the level of everyday conventions, but at another level it does not refer to anything essentially real or ultimately true about me at all. Nationality is a social construct. Likewise, our economic status. Being rich or poor, slave or free: these are socially constructed identities, reflecting the arbitrary circumstances of life, rather than our essential nature. And, of course, the same case is usually made for gender. Male and female may largely be biologically given, but 'masculine' and 'feminine' are usually understood to be social constructs. None of these, or any of our other social identities, can be said to be really real, although we tend to identify with them so closely that we forget ourselves and identify instead with the construct.

In truth, who and what we really are is none of the above, or indeed any of the constructs with which we identify. One of the tasks of a spiritual discipline or meditation practice is to peel

_____

9 Galatians 3.28; Cf. Colossians 3.11

away our various constructs of the self until we are left with . . .
with what? Not nothing surely, for if it means anything to say
we are made in the image and likeness of God, then whatever
we mean by 'God' must be – in some sense – the deepest reality of what we are.[10] What we are left with is, finally, what is.
Meditation is the process by which what Paul calls the 'old
self' – the ordinary, everyday self of ordinary, everyday life,
characterized by anger, malice, greed and so on – is 'stripped
off' and renewed 'according to the image of its creator'.[11] It is
the process by which we become real. And the mark of this
renewal is that the false distinctions of human social constructs
evaporate, for our true nature is neither Jew nor Greek, neither
slave nor free, neither male nor female.

Just as the nature of the God in whose image we are made
is not an object in the world but the very ground of being
itself, so too our essential nature, participating somehow in
the divine nature, is none of the things we attach to or identify with as being I, me or mine. To be made in the image of
a Trinitarian God, whose very being is defined by relational-
ity between 'three persons' who are 'one substance', is to be
'of one being' with one another. The Church is identified as
the body of Christ, and Christians are meant to understand
themselves both as members of that 'one body in Christ' and
'members one of another'.[12] Identity is relational, not absolute;
created not intrinsic. This is as true of people as it is of institutions and, indeed, all things. In other words, an entity – of any
description – is only what it is in relation to and dependent
on what it is not. The deepest reality of what we are is, at
the same time, that which is fundamentally other than what
we normally think of as 'me'. Therefore, the self is nothing in
itself, but only what it is relative to something radically other
than self – whether that is conceived in terms of other people or
the ultimate reality and ground of being that we call God.

---

10 Genesis 1.26-27, 9.6; Cf. Wisdom 2.23, 12.1
11 Colossians 3.9–10
12 Romans 12.5

If the so-called 'inner self', the self as we normally understand and experience ourselves, is not really who and what we
really are, is not really real, then what are we talking about
when we talk about 'the soul'? When we talk about the soul,
we refer not so much to something 'within' a person, some part
of us that is distinct from our body, but rather the whole of our
being, including, paradoxically, all the projections and attachments that are not 'really' our 'true' self. The self is just who and
what we are, in our behaviour, our social relations, our physical, mental and emotional being-in-the-world. It is a label of
convenience. The word 'soul' surely does not refer to some kind
of an entity or substance, but rather that which makes a human
being uniquely human, that which is held in regard. It is a word
that denotes the sacred dimension of human life, an indicator of
human value, a reference to the fundamental truth of our being.
Instead of imagining the soul as a 'thing', therefore, perhaps it
would make more sense to think of it as a quality, like the smell
of a flower: intangible yet unmistakeable. It is not something we
have, an entity that is independent of our experience, so much
as something we are. And we can say that the soul is 'divine' in
the sense that it represents that which is not 'merely' human,
but truly human. And it is eternal and unchanging in the sense
that it is and always will be what makes humans human, as
opposed to animals, plants, rocks or computers. In this way,
therefore, the soul somehow represents the deepest reality of
what we are – whatever that might actually be or mean.

At the heart of being is a mysterious emptiness. It is not possible even to give it a name. I am and I know that I am. This
is the fundamental intuition of being, the irreducible fact of
consciousness. Of that we can be sure. The rest is stories.

Humility

The practice of meditation is often seen as a quest for self-
knowledge. But if the self is not an entity as such, and is without
substance, how then can we come to know it? The cultivation

of self-awareness is not about knowledge of an object, so much as a process of coming to see the patterns of our habits and conditioning for what they are, in order that we might learn to live life more skilfully. This could be described as a kind of 'mental archaeology'. It requires piercing honesty and ruthless determination to sift through the layers of accumulated sediment – the thoughts, feelings, memories and sensations – that make up the propensities that we identify as our self. The first answer will seldom be the right one: we have to keep going until we can go no further.

The idea is to become aware of our own programming, or to see ourselves as others see us. But it requires deep humility to let go of our sense of identification with the false selves that we have constructed, not least because the very habits and conditioned behaviour patterns that we need to expose are the things that we are most accustomed to thinking of as our self. With perseverance, however, we will not only become aware of these habits and patterns – our characteristic mannerisms, favourite turns of phrase, or knee-jerk reactions to particular situations – but we will also be able to see the underlying processes. Some of what we uncover will be the negative and harmful forms of behaviour with which we routinely, if unknowingly, sabotage ourselves and our relationships with others. But only when we are able to see how we act and react out of our conditioning can we begin to free ourselves from its control. Until and unless we do, we will constantly project our own personal issues and agendas onto others, rather than seeing the part we ourselves are playing in the stories going on around us. It is no accident that Jesus talks about a 'log' being lodged in the eye of the one without self-awareness.[13] Hard though it may be, we have to try to see our own blind spot.

Admittedly it is not easy. Our dispositions become us, and we lose the ability to see the difference between what we are and how we act, making us unable to unpick the threads from which our self has been woven. The difficulty is not so much

13 Matthew 7.3–5

47

giving up the ostensible object of attachment or identification – whatever that may be – but letting go of our sense of
being the one who possesses it, and who is therefore defined
and possessed by it. It becomes quite impossible if we cannot
see the patterns of our conditioning for what they are. But by
becoming aware of how we behave, by observing ourselves as
if we were someone else, we may gradually become aware of
the contours of our ingrained tendencies. And because what
we are talking about are essentially patterns of behaviour –
albeit patterns with the appearance of permanence – those
patterns can be analysed, understood and sometimes even
rewritten.

Through the cultivation of self-awareness we discover who
and what we have been constructed as, both in the sense of the
false constructs of our attachments, and also in terms of our true
nature that is the image and likeness of God. The goal of self-
awareness is to understand our behaviour and strive for greater
harmony and integration – with ourselves and others. To be
self-aware is to have a greater degree of self-control, whereas
what we are unaware of controls us. By becoming aware of the
patterns that define us, the habits and masks we have adopted,
we stand a greater chance of gaining a measure of the freedom
that comes with improved self-confidence, which is not to be
confused with being extroverted. Often enough extroversion is
a disguise for lack of self-confidence. True self-confidence is the
outcome of accepting ourselves as we are, regardless of how we
think we would like things to be. It is to be able to choose how
we act, rather than always reacting out of our conditioning.

A spiritual practice is not so much a matter of trying to
change ourselves, but rather letting go of who and what we
think we are, and accepting ourselves as who and what we
really are. We cannot change the self, not least because it is
not any kind of a 'thing' in the first place; but we can become
aware of our programming. Indeed, trying to force change can
be counter-productive, reinforcing the familiar constructs of
the self and further obscuring what lies beneath. This would
be one way of reading the well-known dictum to turn the other

cheek.[14] There is nothing to be gained by resisting evil with evil; it only makes the problem worse. We need to be able to look in the mirror and accept what we see there: neither rejecting it, nor artificially affirming it either. And that mirror is other people. To be self-aware is to observe without identifying. It is to see ourselves as others see us, and to regard others as if they were ourselves. Self-awareness is, literally, to be aware of yourself as if from the point of view of someone else – which is why when we talk about 'feeling self-conscious', what we actually mean is that we feel as if we are the object of another consciousness. It is only when we see the self as other, and the other as self that we know who and what we really are. Coming to know the self through and as 'other' is the meaning of the practice of self-awareness that is more or less common to all spiritual traditions.

The cultivation of self-awareness – and the practice of prayer generally – requires the humility to empty the self of itself, and to be seen by another, as 'other'. Unfortunately, however, humility is one of those awkward words that many people do not seem to like very much these days. Humility is often derided as a negative and unattractive quality, which is all about putting ourselves down. In this self-obsessed and individualistic age, it is viewed with great suspicion as something that is morbidly unhealthy. But the truth is that humility is absolutely vital to the health of any human community and, indeed, personal and social relationships in general. It is the principal antidote to the solipsistic self-centredness that pervades so much of contemporary life, and which fails to take seriously the reality of other people. Without the humility to listen to and engage with the 'other', there can be no genuine contact or communication between us.

Humility is the essential basis of any relationship, whether with other people or with God. And in that relationship, we have to learn that we are not in charge. It is not all about us. Indeed it cannot be all about us if we are truly to engage with

14 Matthew 5.39

the reality of the other. As we all know from our own experience, if one person acts selfishly, putting their own interests before those of the group of which they are a part – and we are all parts of all sorts of groups – it causes immense disruption to everybody else. Living together, sharing a world as we do, requires us sometimes to put the interests of others before our own.[15] This is not about being weak and giving in or putting ourselves down, but being strong enough to ignore the selfish demands of our ego. Humility is not about making ourselves smaller, but being big enough to compromise for the sake of someone else. It is not about denigrating ourselves, or pretending to be worthless, but simply a matter of not showing off or making comparisons between ourselves and others. But it must be genuine. The kind of false humility that contrives to be seen to be doing the right thing is just another ego trip. Genuine humility takes no thought for the self and is thus the only effective remedy for the egocentrism that prevents the establishment of harmonious social and personal relationships. By making us aware that we are not the sole inhabitant of our own private universe, that we are not the only one that matters, humility makes us present to others and thus brings us into the humbling presence of an objective reality that transcends the limitations of our own subjective individuality.

No wonder, then, that Jesus frequently exhorts his disciples to cultivate humility, telling them that the 'first will be last, and the last will be first'.[16] Far from diminishing the self, humility actually leads to its true fulfilment. This is why, in promising the ultimate freedom, Jesus demands the ultimate sacrifice – the two must go together. 'If any want to become my followers,' he says, 'let them deny themselves and take up their cross and follow me. For those who want to save their life will lose it, and those who lose their life for my sake will find it.'[17] For him,

---

15 1 Corinthians 10.24
16 Matthew 19.30, 20.16; Mark 9.35, 10.31; Luke 13.30
17 Matthew 16.24–5, 10.39; Mark 8.34–5; Luke 9.23–44, 17.33;
Cf. John 12.25

that meant death on a cross; for the rest of us, it means laying aside the self in order to reveal God. Letting go of self-interest, putting aside the ego, giving up our illusions: these are the necessary foundations for awakening.

Humility is also – as it happens – the basis of love, for we can only truly love when we abandon our egocentric agenda and cultivate the self-awareness that is the awareness of others. When Jesus says we must lose our self to find our self, he is saying we must give up our illusions, our concepts, beliefs, opinions, identifications and attachments. It is these that must die. Moreover, the projected self has to die in order for awakening to be possible, just as Moses had to die before the Israelites could reach the Promised Land.[18] Indeed, the death of falsehood is awakening. Jesus teaches us to die to our old life – the life that is death – in order to be born anew, into the life that is truly life itself. Paradoxically, self-knowledge requires self-denial. By understanding the true nature of self, the false self disappears and we become who and what we really are. The discipline of meditation is the process by which we die to the old self, to all our concepts and opinions, our attachments and identifications in order to be born anew, awake and free. This is why Paul describes baptism – the rite of initiation into the Christian life – in terms of the death of the old, and the birth of the new. To die to sin is to live to God.[19]

Understanding the nature of the self is arguably the most important aspect of the awakening we strive towards in meditation. As we peel away one personality construct after another, revealing the fundamental intuition of being that is the deepest reality of what we are, we slowly start to arise from our dreamy slumber. Not, I hasten to add, that there is anyone who wakes up, or even anywhere to wake up to. To be awake means to be aware in the dream that one is a dream entity, dreaming. We are all asleep, but occasionally we may become aware that we are asleep. That is the only difference, the most we can

---

18 Deuteronomy 32.51
19 Romans 6.8, 10–11; Cf. Philippians 3

hope for. To be 'awake', even in this limited sense, however, is enough to be able see through some of the illusions in which we are trapped. To be awake is no longer to be a sleepwalker stumbling blindly through life and bumping into everything. It is to break free from our conditioning, from all that controls us. We may have no choice but to play the game, but at least we can play knowing it is a game.

4

Not Peace But a Sword

People often tell me they would like to meditate but do not have the time. There may be circumstances in which this is undoubtedly the case, but more often than not it comes across as a rather feeble excuse. The truth is we have little problem making time for the things we really want to do. Of course, there could be very good reasons why we genuinely find it hard to make time for our spiritual practice. But as with anything else in life, it is a question of how we set our priorities. If we are sufficiently motivated, we will find the time somehow, even if we have to make some compromises. Admittedly, it helps to have access to somewhere quiet and it helps to be able to set aside a period of time that is not going to be interrupted. And for anyone with a young family, or a demanding job, this may be virtually impossible; although if all our time is already taken up, then that in itself should prompt us to reflect on our use of time. This in turn may be the first step towards re-evaluating our priorities and modifying our lifestyle to make it more conducive to a spiritual practice. If we say we have no time, it is time to look at how we use our time, and to ask ourselves whether we have the balance right. How much of that time do we use productively? And how much do we waste? We routinely 'kill time' in all sorts of ways, often without even realizing it. Can we really afford to be so extravagant?

Having said that, the aspiration to establish a regular pattern of practice amid the busyness of everyday life can at times seem like an unreachable goal, both for the beginner and the experienced practitioner alike. Being unable to find the time to meditate may be all it takes to prevent us from undertaking any kind of spiritual practice whatsoever. If we are sufficiently determined, however, it should be possible to make one or two small changes to our normal routine that will allow us to create the necessary foundations of a sustainable discipline. For example, would it be possible to get up half an hour earlier? Or to reconsider how you start the day? Perhaps you listen to the news on the radio when the alarm goes off in the morning. Perhaps you have the television on while you eat breakfast. Perhaps you check your emails while sipping that first cup of coffee. It would be much easier to create the necessary conditions – not to mention time – for meditation by simply not doing those things, by starting the day with a period of quietness instead. There will be plenty of opportunities to catch up on the news and answer emails; and it is always much easier to meditate before the mind has been swamped with all the busyness of daily life.

Creating a little space in our lives for reflective quietness need not be as difficult as it may at first appear, but we do have to want to do it. The ability to prioritize is one of the most useful skills in life in general, and it is certainly necessary in the spiritual life. It is no coincidence that some of the most committed practitioners of meditation are also among the busiest of people, whether they are working parents with demanding children, or high-powered business executives. The reason they cope well and are successful in what they do is because they manage their time and they work hard. They work hard because they are disciplined. And, very often, they are disciplined – not to mention capable of being both detached and focused at the same time – because they meditate. They have learned that setting aside time apparently to 'do nothing' actually makes them better able to think clearly and act effectively. Taking time out to meditate is precisely what enables them to get more done. This is also, of course, why meditation is so often billed as an antidote to stress – the feeling of not having enough time to do everything that needs to be done.

In the Ten Commandments given by God to Moses on Mount Sinai, the great importance of keeping the Sabbath – a time to rest, to step back and do nothing – is indicated by the fact that it is listed immediately after the primary injunctions against idolatry and blasphemy, and before the rules of ethical conduct. The commandment to keep a day of rest is a requirement to be still, to allow God into our lives and hearts. It is so important that noncompliance is punishable with death.[1] And indeed, we surely will die spiritually if we do not take time out to connect with the deepest reality of what we are, or that which is God. Meditation is a deliberate effort to create the space necessary for the spirit to flourish, and – as a welcome by-product – it will very often provide the appropriate vantage point from which to resolve whatever issues we may be dealing with as well. Far from making us cold and distant, taking a step back from ourselves and our concerns actually enables us to be more engaged. Stepping back and putting things into perspective makes it easier to see the whole, and to make balanced decisions. Sometimes we need to cultivate a bit of detachment – particularly when it comes to personal and emotional matters – in order to be more objective. This kind of detachment, which is not to be confused with indifference, is essential to the practice of meditation. When Jesus declared that 'prophets are not without honour, except in their home town, and among their own kin' he was alerting us to the profound truth that if we enter seriously into the spiritual life, we will inevitably find ourselves to some extent set apart from 'the world'.[2]

Discipline

Managing time, setting priorities and putting things into perspective all require a certain amount of discipline. Above all, we need discipline when it comes to meditation because – if we are

---

1 Exodus 31.12–17
2 Mark 6.4; Matthew 13.57; John 4.44

honest with ourselves – much of the time we do not really feel like doing it. Much of the time it is difficult, and often it is simply boring. And we will always be able to think of something more important that we ought to be doing instead. But this can be true of anything in life. Like anything worthwhile, cultivating a spiritual practice takes effort: a degree of strictness is necessary, rather like pruning a plant in order to stimulate its growth. Having said that, our discipline should not be excessive. If we force ourselves to undertake a discipline that is too severe, or engage in exercises that are too strenuous, it could impair our health and make it impossible to maintain any kind of practice at all. Extremes of discipline can be harmful in other ways too. Showing off with displays of immoderate asceticism suggests pride rather than piety. Jesus made it very clear that those who seek to gain the approval of others on account of their supposed spiritual expertise have 'had their reward'.[3] A pat on the back might make us feel good about ourselves, but that is all it will do. It will not bring about genuine transformation. In fact, it will impede our spiritual growth. Therefore, a properly balanced discipline should be understood as a middle way, neither repressive nor indulgent. The purpose of discipline, in the spiritual life, is not to punish the body but to purify the mind.

In this context, discipline has two aspects: individual and corporate. One of the best ways to understand the need for corporate discipline – in life in general, as well as the spiritual life – is to remember that we are not isolated, autonomous individuals. Human beings are social animals; we exist in relation to others, as members of groups and communities. And in any kind of group or community, it is some form of discipline that enables people who may not have chosen to associate with each other, or who otherwise have little in common, to work together or live alongside one another in relative harmony. Discipline is about taking responsibility for our being-in-the-world, while the lack of it is a critical factor in much of the social disintegration we see in contemporary society. In this context, discipline is not

---

3 Matthew 6.1–2

restrictive but rather that which makes the life of a community possible in the first place. We see this most clearly perhaps in monastic communities, governed as they are by detailed rules of life explicitly designed to facilitate communal living, but it is also true for the rest of us, because we all belong to groups and communities of one sort or another. Contrary to the popular view of discipline as an oppressive infringement of our liberty, the truth is that discipline is actually what makes freedom possible. Interestingly, the problem here is not that we do not understand the need for discipline – we have no trouble with discipline when it concerns something we want to do – but rather that we do not understand the nature of freedom.

The spiritual life is often described in terms of an aspiration to freedom. Indeed, the desire for freedom is arguably one of our strongest motivations in life. We instinctively yearn to be free. But what actually is this freedom that we all want? It seems widely to be assumed that freedom is synonymous with freedom of choice, which in turn implies having a measure of control over our circumstances. And in the consumer society, choice is the trademark of the fully realized individual. But this is an illusion. Our choices are pre-determined for us. Far from being a recipe for happiness, so-called freedom of choice feeds the delusions of control that render us powerless and unable to make our own decisions. Ironically, the more choice we have, the more helpless and inadequate we feel. Keeping our options open leads not to freedom but frustration, indecision, and fear of missing out on more attractive alternatives. And so we meekly collude with the myth that life would be so much better if only we could buy into the dream. This is not freedom. True freedom is not the freedom to indulge our every whim, but freedom from the slavery to our programmed desire for self-gratification. Strange as it may initially seem, freedom is defined by what limits it. Paradoxically, therefore, discipline is actually the basis of freedom: it is the 'narrow gate' that leads to fullness of life.[4]

---

4 Matthew 7.13–14; Cf. John 10.10

Not only is freedom defined by what limits it, but it also comes with responsibilities. This is something that people very often forget – especially those who define freedom in terms of choice or the absence of externally imposed rules and regulations. We live in a culture in which the autonomous right of the individual to seek his or her own fulfilment has become the highest good; being true to oneself is all that matters. But what does it mean to be true to oneself if that 'truth' does not include a sense of responsibility for the well-being – and freedom – of others? The spiritual life is all about the cultivation of self-awareness, but this can sometimes lead to the mistaken view that it is therefore preoccupied with the self. This impression is not helped by the emphasis in some forms of contemporary spirituality on self-improvement and personal fulfilment. But there is a big difference between being self-aware and being self-obsessed. It may be true in one sense that the self is the only reality we know, and that in the end we are alone; but it is also the case that the opposite is true: we are what we are by virtue of our relationships with others. No attempt to cultivate self-awareness can ignore the reality of the other, and the need to take responsibility for the consequences of our actions, which is why the popular notion of being spiritual but not religious is so fundamentally incoherent. A religion is not just a tedious list of things we must and must not do, but rather that which binds us – as the etymology of the word suggests – in relationships of commitment and accountability: both to that which is God, and to each other. Personal spirituality cannot be divorced from social responsibility and moral conduct in relation to those with whom we share our world. Individual and corporate discipline are inseparable.

A spiritual practice thus implies an ethical practice, or moral discipline. It is no accident that the religion of Israel was founded on the basis of the Law given by God to Moses on Mount Sinai.[5] The Ten Commandments remind us that the ethical life is absolutely fundamental to the spiritual life,

---

5 Exodus 20.1–17

and we see the same emphasis in other traditions too. Virtuous living is not an added extra, or something commended for 'ordinary' people but not the 'elect'. The first Christians realized that following Jesus meant following the example of his conduct. 'Whoever says, "I abide in him", ought to walk just as he walked.'[6] Without the solid basis of an ethical discipline, and the social responsibility it implies, no spiritual path is possible – a point made very clear by Jesus, who came not to abolish the Law, but to fulfil it.[7] The spiritual life and the ethical life are inextricably linked: the value of the former will be assessed by its moral outcomes, which is why Jesus tells us that we ought to judge people 'by their fruits'.[8] If the fruit of one's spiritual practice is not apparent in one's behaviour towards others, then what good is it? 'Bear fruit worthy of repentance,' cried John the Baptist.[9] If our spirituality does not awaken within us a profound sense of personal humility, compassion and respect for others; if it does not make us better people, and the world a better place, then it is worthless.

Corporate discipline and personal discipline sustain and enable each other. For example, many people will appreciate the advantages of meditating in a group. Being part of a group imposes a discipline that encourages us in our own practice. But we also need a degree of personal discipline in order to function as part of a group in the first place. So although discipline is, for many people, a word that conjures up negative connotations of punishment and repression, we should remember that it comes from the Latin *disciplina*, which has meanings to do with instruction and learning. Hence, in ordinary language we also use it to refer to a skill, training or field of expertise. And indeed, this is the understanding of discipline that we encounter in the Bible. The Letter to

---

6 1 John 2.6
7 Matthew 5.17–18; Cf. 22.36–40
8 Matthew 7.16, 20
9 Matthew 3.8; Luke 3.8

the Hebrews concedes that, 'discipline always seems painful rather than pleasant at the time, but later it yields the peaceful fruit of righteousness to those who have been trained by it'.[10] The word most commonly used to refer to spiritual discipline is asceticism, which, like any other kind of discipline, has a simple rationality: the sacrifice of present enjoyment for the sake of a greater reward in the future. Anyone who has studied for an examination, gone on a diet, or trained in order to get fit, is already familiar with the basic principle. Indeed the term 'asceticism' derives from the Greek word for physical exercise, which is why Paul draws a parallel between spiritual exercise and athletic training.[11]

The cultivation of self-awareness entails radical personal transformation, and that is not something that just happens overnight. What is more, it may even come as a bit of a shock to the system. We will find that it is hard to change the habits of a lifetime, just as we often find it hard to learn a new skill. It can be difficult to muster the discipline and motivation we need in order to engage in a spiritual practice: all the more so when we take into account the demanding work commitments and family responsibilities that are such an important part of everyday life for many people. But the discipline and motivation necessary for spiritual practice are really no different to the discipline and motivation needed to go on a diet, give up smoking, take more exercise or pursue a hobby – all things that most people are able to manage if and when they really want to. I know full well that I should eat less and exercise more, and admittedly it is quite difficult at times to make myself do it; any excuse will be sufficient to put me off. But it is possible. It can be done. Spiritual discipline is no different.

Like physical exercise, spiritual discipline involves a process that a part of us may be unwilling to undergo. Like physical exercise, spiritual discipline can be off-putting: all the more

10 Hebrews 12.11
11 1 Corinthians 9.25

so when it involves participation in a corporate practice, such as attending church. But one thing we ought to realize about being part of a faith community, or any similar group, is that it is not simply a cosy gathering of the likeminded but a workshop of the spirit in which identities and relationships are tried, tested and transformed, just as the Israelites were in the wilderness.[12] The Church exists not so that it can be moulded to our purposes, but rather so that we can be moulded to God's purposes. It is an arena in which egos collide and personalities jostle against each other. Our participation in such a body is a core element of the discipline by which we grow in spiritual awareness, or godliness, and are formed in the likeness of Christ. In our practice we need the support of others – that great cloud of witnesses spoken of by the author of the Letter to the Hebrews – not only to support and encourage us, but also to hold us to account.[13] The spiritual life is not a soft option. It invariably involves friction, conflict, trials and endurance. Sparks fly and passions burn. It can even bring out the worst in us, like poison from an infected wound. But in a strange way, this is how it should be, because a spiritual discipline is a furnace in which the soul is refined, purified and ultimately recreated.[14] 'Blessed is anyone who endures temptation,' says the author of the Letter of James. 'Such a one has stood the test and will receive the crown of life that the Lord has promised to those who love him.'[15]

Uncomfortable though the process may sometimes be, the reward of spiritual practice is truly beyond all price, for it is nothing less than 'the life that really is life'.[16] This is the radical and profoundly life-threatening transformation implied in one of the most haunting of the many difficult sayings attributed to

---

12 Deuteronomy 8.2
13 Hebrews 12.1
14 Job 36.21; Psalm 66.10; Judith 8.27; Wisdom 3.6
15 James 1.12
16 1 Timothy 6.19

Jesus: 'I have not come to bring peace, but a sword.'[17] We are likely to find these challenging words all the more awkward to hear when confronted by the common accusation that religion is responsible for all the world's conflict, division and oppression. At first it seems deeply shocking to hear Jesus, the Prince of Peace, appearing to promote violence and conflict. Yet, if we read the Gospels, we will have to admit that everywhere he goes he stirs up in people their deepest fears and insecurities. Jesus demands of those who would be his disciples that they turn their backs on the world, their friends and family.[18] He threatens their cosy illusions and attachments – and, therefore, ours too. Entering into the spiritual life requires a complete re-evaluation of everything we have previously taken for granted. It challenges our most basic assumptions, and undermines our fragile sense of security in the 'things of the world'. In a very real sense, then, embarking upon the spiritual journey brings not peace but discord, not life but death: the death of our illusions of self.

If nothing else, this emphasis on the struggle that is an inevitable part of any spiritual discipline soon puts paid to the popular notion many people seem to have that spirituality or religion is a bit of a 'comfort blanket', a helpful delusion to make us feel better about ourselves. A quick glance at the biography of any great religious figure will soon show that their prophetic call to radical social and personal transformation invariably involves gargantuan effort and enormous personal sacrifice. And indeed, I am sure that many of us have in our own lives faced difficult moments on account of our faith, not least the ridicule of family, friends or work colleagues. The truth is, there is nothing easy about the spiritual life. Taken with the seriousness it truly demands it may be one of the most challenging enterprises we are ever likely to undertake, for it requires nothing less than that we give up our precious notions of who and what we think we are in order to become who and what we really are. Far

---

17 Matthew 10.34
18 Mathew 10.37; Luke 14.26; Cf. Luke 9.61–62

from being a crutch, following the spiritual path forces us to throw away our crutches, and take a sword to much that we may previously have thought important, including – or perhaps, especially – ourselves.[19]

This image of struggle and conflict presents a sharp contrast with much contemporary popular spirituality, where the emphasis often seems to be on self-help and the fulfilment of our emotional needs and desires, implying in turn that it is only meant for people with problems. This is not to say that the spiritual life is not about wholeness and healing – of course it is: the Bible contains dozens of references to the healing power of God – but the wholeness in question is predicated on healing the breach in our separation from God, the ground of our being. The 'problem' we are here to solve is not our lack of personal or emotional fulfilment but the underlying cause of our existential suffering, the profound and all-pervasive unsatisfactoriness of the human condition encapsulated in the notion of 'original sin'. Jesus calls us in no uncertain terms to 'Repent, and believe in the good news.'[20] To repent is to turn away from sin – the unskilful living that is the consequence of not seeing things the way they are – and return to God, or that which is ultimately real and true. This means giving up self-centredness and living instead for something that is other than self, namely that which is God. The resolution of personal problems may well be part of that, but it is surely not the point of it. The point is waking up, which also, as it happens, resolves everything else as well.

Spirituality is not about how God can be used to serve my needs, for this would be to make God into just another lifestyle choice, a consumer product re-branded as an intimate experience of myself, for a society in which the notion of 'sin' – or living in and through the ego – is no longer regarded as a problem. It is rather about how I can serve God and thus become more in tune with the way things are. By reducing spirituality

19 Matthew 10.39, 16.25; Mark 8.35; Luke 9.24, 17.33; John 12.25
20 Mark 1.15

to therapy, focusing on the personal rather than the universal, we subordinate God to our own agenda; evidence – if any were needed – that we live not so much in a secular culture as an idolatrous one. If the sole purpose of our practice is to attend to our personal issues, we risk mistaking the map for the territory it represents. The salvation that Jesus promises to those who follow him requires us to renounce the gods of our own making, to turn away from ourselves towards something beyond, something fundamentally other than self. 'I have come not to bring peace but a sword,' says Jesus, inverting the egocentric values of the world, turning us literally inside out and pointing us towards what really matters. By answering the call to follow the spiritual path, we are in danger of having our lives turned completely upside down. But we also make ourselves open to the possibility of true liberation.

Renunciation

The Bible presents a stark challenge to the narcissistic individualism of our contemporary consumer culture, calling us to seek not our own interests but that which is God. In common with the spiritual teachings of many other religious traditions, the message seems to be that if we wish to attain true fulfilment then a part of us must, paradoxically, be given up. Following the spiritual path, engaging in the practice of meditation, is thus the supreme act of faith because, on this journey, we must ultimately leave ourselves behind.

Renunciation lies at the heart of many of the world's great spiritual traditions. It certainly lies at the heart of the gospels, full as they are of teachings about how we must give up wealth and money and riches if we want to be saved. Whoever does not hate 'even life itself, cannot be my disciple', says Jesus, before adding, 'none of you can become my disciple if you do not give up all your possessions.'[21] This way of thinking seems

---

21 Luke 14.26, 33; Cf. Luke 12.15

so contrary to the spirit of the age – perhaps the spirit of every age – which is why these words are as fresh and as challenging today as they must have been 2000 years ago. Jesus commands those who would be his disciples to renounce worldly wealth and earthly glory, for 'what will it profit them to gain the whole world and forfeit their life?'[22] He tells us that 'it is easier for a camel to go through the eye of a needle than for someone who is rich to enter the kingdom of God'.[23] The message is clear: 'You cannot serve God and wealth.'[24] If we wish to be saved, we must give all we have to the poor and needy.[25] Rather than amassing worldly wealth for ourselves, we are to store up treasure in heaven, 'where neither moth nor rust consumes'.[26] Ultimately, 'the world' cannot deliver true and lasting satisfaction: we should instead be seeking the kingdom, or what really matters.[27]

Renunciation is a theme that recurs again and again throughout the Bible. It is present in explicit directives, as we see in the teachings of Jesus, and it can also be discerned under the guise of allegory and metaphor, such as in the story of the institution of the Passover in the Book of Exodus. This marks the decisive point at which the Israelites break away from their life of slavery in Egypt, and begin their journey to the Promised Land: the goal of ultimate fulfilment, freedom and salvation. The Passover thus represents the traumatic event that brings about their spiritual awakening; its bloodthirsty narrative of the killing of the firstborn of the Egyptians symbolizes the death of the ego, the lower self, to which we are enslaved. But as we know only too well from our own experience, the ego does not give up so easily. We might renounce the world, but that does not mean the world will relinquish its claim on us. The Israelites

---

22 Mark 8.36; Cf. Matthew 16.26; Luke 9.25
23 Matthew 19.24; Mark 10.25; Luke 18.25
24 Luke 16.13; Cf. Psalm 52.7
25 Matthew 19.21; Mark 10.21; Luke 18.22; Cf. Tobit 12.8–9
26 Matthew 6.20–1; Luke 12.33–4; Cf. Luke 12.16–21
27 Matthew 13.44–6

were immediately pursued by Pharaoh and his army, just as we may be pursued by 'the world' as it tries to claw us back. The Egyptian army, however, is drowned in the sea while the Israelites pass through safely.[28] This crossing marks the point of no return, as it represents the death of the old self, and – after passage through the waters – birth of the new.

Spiritual renunciation apparently requires us to embrace poverty, detachment and humility, in order first to reject and then to transcend the self-serving domination of the ego. But what is it we are actually required to give up: our wealth and material possessions, or our sense of personal identification with them? The stark message found throughout the Gospels – and in much of the rest of the Bible too, for that matter – is quite clear: 'life does not consist in the abundance of possessions'.[29] The comforts and pleasures of this world, as the prophet Amos points out – the 'beds of ivory' and the 'idle songs' that entertain us – cannot provide true joy and freedom because, like the 'revelry of the loungers', they too shall pass away.[30] Renunciation should be understood not only in relation to our material possessions and wealth, therefore, but also our opinions, values, aspirations and vested interests. After all, the problem is not money as such, but the love of money – investing our happiness in the attainment of wealth for its own sake – and the 'many senseless and harmful desires that plunge people into ruin and destruction'.[31] Paul is talking here about spiritual ruin and destruction, primarily, but if we think about it, greed is generally ruinous in whatever form it appears. An inordinate desire for wealth is almost certainly guaranteed to result in moral and spiritual poverty. There is really no way of making this fundamental truth more palatable, cutting as it does to the very core of much that we hold dear. And what applies to

---

28 Exodus 14
29 Luke 12.15
30 Amos 6.4–7; Cf. Proverbs 27.24; James 5.1–3
31 1 Timothy 6.9–10; Cf. Hebrews 13.5

individuals, applies also to whole societies – as is readily apparent in the world today.

We belong to a society in which we tend to define ourselves in terms of our possessions: the things we buy and imagine we own are fundamental to our sense of self. This applies not only to physical things, but anything we claim as ours, including our beliefs, views, desires and preferences. Thus when Jesus demands that we give up our possessions, it is not so much the objects themselves that represent the problem but our identification with or attachment to them.[32] In other words, the self that is identified with the things of the world is not our true self, made in the image and likeness of God but an idol of our own fabrication, which mars the image of God within us. The desire for wealth thus represents a powerful delusion in the human psyche. It fosters the illusion that we are actually the owners or possessors of the things we think we own and possess, that they somehow constitute our identity, and that through them we can have some sort of control over the contingencies of life.

This is pure fantasy. The truth is, of course, that we do not really own anything – because there is no owner – and we have almost no control whatsoever over the contingencies of human existence.[33] As Paul so succinctly points out, 'we brought nothing into this world, so that we can take nothing out of it'.[34] The point he is making here is not simply that we brought nothing in and it also happens to be the case that we take nothing out, but rather it is because we brought nothing in, therefore we cannot take anything out. The implication being that our essential nature does not subsist in the things we think we own, the things in which we mistakenly invest our identity. Paul describes the love of money as the root of all evil because it leads us into other sins, such as avarice, greed and so on. By feeding the illusion that we can control and even dictate the circumstances of life, the lure of wealth swells the ego and

---

32 Matthew 19.21; Mark 10.21; Luke 12.15, 33; 14.33; 18.22
33 Luke 12.20
34 1 Timothy 6.7; Cf. Psalm 49.17

poisons the soul, making us think that we are more important or powerful than others.

In a story that appears only in Luke's Gospel, we have a variation on this pivotal theme of self-sacrifice and renunciation. Zacchaeus, a tax collector, that most despised class of people in Jewish society, a man who had made himself rich by stealing from his fellow countrymen on behalf of the hated Roman forces of occupation, is – to the horror of those standing by – befriended by Jesus, who basically invites himself round for tea.[35] Not surprisingly, this is considered to be absolutely scandalous. How could Jesus accept the hospitality of such an outcast? But of course, Jesus is concerned to seek the lost: to save sinners, not the righteous. After all, it is a sick person who needs a doctor, not someone in good health.[36] As a result of his encounter with Jesus, Zacchaeus decides to mend his ways, resolving to redistribute his ill-gotten gains, and to repay – with interest – those whom he has cheated. Here we see clearly the relationship between renunciation, repentance and redemption that is so central to the gospel message. The first stage of any spiritual undertaking must begin with repentance, turning away from self towards that which is God, as we respond to the wake-up call alerting us to the fact that all is not as it should be. Repentance becomes renunciation, as we learn to give up our identification with the objects and idols of this world, be they material or mental, in order to invest our sense of self and what really matters in that which is ultimately real and true, represented by the notion of 'treasure in heaven'.[37] From here the path of purification leads us to redemption: the freedom from egocentrism or sin that is the hope of life eternal, life not in the delusions of the self but the ultimate reality of the divine transcendent other we call God.

It is interesting to compare the story of Zacchaeus with the story of the rich young man, which occurs in all three synoptic

---

35 Luke 19.1–10
36 Matthew 9.12; Mark 2.17; Luke 5.31
37 Matthew 6.21; 19.21; Mark 10.21; Luke 12.34; 18.22

gospels, because there is something similar about the theme –
redemption through repentance and renunciation – even though
the two stories have very different outcomes.[38] The rich young
man comes to Jesus and says, 'Teacher, what good deed must
I do to have eternal life?' Or, in other words, 'what must I do
to attain salvation, or perfect freedom?' After all, 'eternal life'
represents the ultimate freedom – not just from mortality, but
also from the prison of our ego or constructed self. Eternal
life is real life, free from webs of vanity and delusion. It is life
from the perspective of that which is ultimately real and ultimately true. The answer Jesus gives may not be what we expect.
He says, 'If you wish to be perfect, go, sell your possessions,
and give the money to the poor, and you will have treasure in
heaven; then come, follow me.' Clearly this was not what the
rich young man who asked the question wanted to hear.

Freedom is not based on the seductive illusions of control,
but the renunciation of illusions of self. If you want to go all
the way – to take the path of perfection – you have to give it all
up – even, or in fact especially, your self. The rich young man
was a prisoner to his possessions, and the notions of selfhood
that they engendered, unable to see that true freedom does not
depend on having enough money to be able to do whatever
we want, but quite the opposite. Wealth – which here refers
not only to material goods but whatever we invest with value
and thus use to create our sense of who and what we are – is
more likely to inhibit our freedom and bind us in chains of
self-deception, ignorance and sin. By contrast, to invest our
'treasure' in 'heaven' is to identify with what really matters,
that which is not transient – like the things of this world – but
eternal. 'You reap whatever you sow,' says Paul to the Galatians.
'If you sow to your own flesh, you will reap corruption from
the flesh; but if you sow to the Spirit, you will reap eternal life
from the Spirit.'[39]

---

38 Matthew 19.16–22; Mark 10.17–22; Luke 18.18–23
39 Galatians 6.7–8; Cf. Romans 5.21, 6.23; 1 John 1.2, 5.11–13;
Jude 1.21

The great power of the story of the rich young man is that –
as is so often the case with these narratives – the rich young
man represents all of us, in one way or another. Like him, we
tend to associate freedom with wealth; in the naive belief that
to be free is to be able to do whatever we want, which of course
in this world usually costs money. Wealth is therefore routinely linked with happiness, a fantasy the advertising industry
depends upon for its very existence. But Jesus says that in fact
the very opposite is true. The attainment of freedom requires us
to give up our wealth, because wealth does not – cannot – bring
true and lasting contentment.[40] And, of course, our 'wealth' is
not just to be measured by our financial assets, though this is
the most obvious form it takes. Even though we may not be
especially rich, it is probable that we will still own much that
we consider valuable including all those things – whatever they
may be, whether material or non-material – from which our
sense of self is constructed. Indeed, our wealth might not have
anything to do with physical possessions at all. For example,
we might be very proud of our professional achievements, or
our skills and talents. We might be very attached to the views,
beliefs and opinions that we hold dear. If so, this is what constitutes our 'wealth', because our wealth is that in which we
invest our identity, and by which we are in some sense bound.
And there will be many other forms of wealth that we value,
and will have to give up if we wish to know true freedom. It is
for this reason that Paul exhorts us not to set our hopes on 'the
uncertainty of riches, but rather on God', striving instead to be
'rich in good works' so that we may 'take hold of the life that
really is life'.[41]

Of course, when the rich young man hears what Jesus has
to say to him, he goes away grieving, 'for he had many possessions'. Now, what is interesting about the rich young man,
as compared with Zacchaeus the hated tax collector, is that
he is a well-intentioned, virtuous and upright citizen. He is,

---

40 Ecclesiastes 5.10; Proverbs 27.24
41 1 Timothy 6.17–19

by the conventional standards of his day – and quite unlike Zacchaeus – a 'good person' in the eyes of the world. He keeps the commandments, he fulfils his duty, he does what is expected of him. Nevertheless, he lacks sufficient faith to do the one thing that really matters. After being told what he must do to attain everlasting or real life – after a glimpse of the truth revealed by Jesus – he turns his back and walks away, unable to give up his self, his wealth and his world. He is full of good intentions, but unable to do the one thing necessary to save his soul. As a result, he remains unchanged by his encounter with Jesus.

Zacchaeus, on the other hand, hated and despised – the lowest of the low – is radically transformed as a consequence of meeting Jesus. In contrast to the rich young man, he sees Jesus and he is instantly struck by a profound insight into the way things are. Without needing to be told what he should do, he decides there and then to give away half his possessions to charity – he renounces self-interest, in other words – and resolves to give priority to the needs of others, by making amends to those he has wronged. As a result he is, quite literally, a changed person. No longer an outcast, he is declared by Jesus to be a son of Abraham, one of God's chosen people. By giving up what he held dear, Zacchaeus gains true freedom: just as Jesus promises when he says that if we want to live we must give up our life.[42] He comes with a sword, and we must take that sword to ourselves. True faith is not a possession, not something we have, like beliefs or opinions. It is predicated on giving up our illusions of self.

If we are not changed – radically, profoundly changed – as a result of encountering the word of God, then we are just not listening.

---

42 Matthew 10.39, 16.25; Mark 8.35; Luke 9.24, 17.33; John 12.25

5

When You Pray

Prayer is the essence of the spiritual life. Not surprisingly, the Bible makes frequent mention of people praying. It also contains a fair number of prayers. But it has very little to say about how to pray and it is strangely – or perhaps appropriately – silent when it comes to the subject of meditation and contemplative prayer. This is in spite of the fact that Jesus was clearly in the habit of seeking God in solitude, as were Old Testament prophets such as Moses and Elijah before him. In Mark's Gospel we are told that Jesus got up early one morning before dawn, while it was still dark and the rest of the world was fast asleep. He then 'went out to a deserted place, and there he prayed'.[1] Luke tells us that from time to time 'he would withdraw to deserted places and pray'.[2] Although we do not know exactly what he did when he prayed, there is much that we can infer from the account we have in Matthew's Gospel of Jesus teaching his disciples about prayer.[3]

Even though it is only a few verses, this is probably the most comprehensive treatment of the subject anywhere in the Bible. Indeed, it is one of the very few instances where prayer is discussed in any detail at all. Jesus begins with a stern warning. 'Beware of practising your piety before others in order to be seen by them . . . do not be like the hypocrites.'[4] He then goes on to tell his listeners what they should do instead. 'But

---

1 Mark 1.35; Cf. 6.46; Matthew 14.23
2 Luke 5.16; Cf. 6.12; 9.18
3 Matthew 6.5–13; Cf. Luke 11.1–4
4 Matthew 6.1, 5; Cf. Mark 12.40; Luke 20.47

whenever you pray,' he says, 'go into your room and shut the door and pray to your Father who is in secret; and your Father who sees in secret will reward you.'[5] In this single verse, Jesus encapsulates the practice of contemplative prayer in a simple but concise formula. It can be divided into four parts. First, 'go into your room'; second, 'shut the door'; third, 'pray to your Father who is in secret', and, finally, 'your Father who sees in secret will reward you'.

When we pray, says Jesus, we must first go into our room. This should be understood both literally and metaphorically and as having both an outer and an inner meaning. When we meditate we may indeed go into an actual room, which has been set aside for that purpose, just as when we participate in religious activities we go to a church or some other building specifically designed for the performance of sacred rites. But we can also understand 'going into our room' figuratively in terms of the need for discipline, and a firm resolve to create the inner conditions necessary for our practice. To 'go into your room' can therefore refer to a determination to make space in our lives for meditation. This implies a certain degree of withdrawal from the activity and concerns of everyday life in order to spend some time being still and silent. The notion of going into a room is thus as much about a physical space and practical circumstances, as it is about an interior space and the cultivation of quietness within. We see this in the Exodus story too. After a period in the wilderness, during which the Israelites have grumbled and complained about the hardships of the journey, been distracted by idolatry and received the discipline of the Law, God commands Moses to build him a sanctuary.[6] This is exactly what the discipline of a spiritual practice, or the notion of 'going into our room', entails. We need not only to engineer circumstances conducive to meditation, such as by setting aside a time and a place for it, but also, by means of our

---

5 Matthew 6.6
6 Exodus 25.8

73

practice, we need to create an inner sanctuary, a special place within where we might, like Moses, meet with God.

Having gone into our room, Jesus says we are to shut the door. Again, this should be understood both literally and meta-phorically. The notion of shutting the door suggests the need to minimize the possibility of distraction or interruption, and indeed, there is no doubt that it helps to be somewhere quiet when we meditate, especially to begin with. After temporarily removing ourselves from our normal involvement in the activ-ity of the world by 'going into a room', the next step – shutting the door – requires the withdrawal of our senses, including the mind, from contact with their objects. 'Shutting the door' is, therefore, about denying the mind its usual stimulation, thus making it easier to regulate our attention and cultivate men-tal stillness. In other words, it is a conscious intention not to engage with the sights and sounds around us, or – more import-antly – the thoughts within us. Shutting the door is a meta-phor for the practice of awareness. To shut the door is to try to anchor our attention and keep the mind from wandering. Taken together, going into our room and shutting the door are the necessary foundations that enable meditation or contem-plation to occur.

Once we have established a degree of stillness, by 'going into our room' and 'shutting the door' – which we might also describe in terms of 'sitting quietly' – meditation proper begins. Jesus says we are to pray to our Father 'who is in secret'. The notion of a God who is 'in secret' suggests that God is not an entity that can be named, or circumscribed by our linguistic definitions. God is nothing we can say about 'him'. In this sense God is 'in secret', dwelling 'within', or hidden from us. God is a truth whose form is unknown, whose nature is stillness, peace and calm. The prophet Elijah encountered God in 'a sound of sheer silence' (or the more familiar 'still small voice' of the King James Version).[7] If we would commune with the ultimate real-ity that is being itself, the truth beyond words – which speaks

7 1 Kings 19.12

therefore in 'silence' – then likewise we must be silent if we wish to hear him 'speak' his truth. We must, in the words of the Psalms, 'Be still, and know that I am God.'[8] Contemplative prayer, or meditation, is thus the act of waiting on God in silence.[9] If we would know God, then we must stop talking and learn instead to be quiet and listen, to be 'silent before the Lord God'.[10] Meditation is about listening to God – tuning in to reality as it really is – and God responds in silence, in secret. God is met in silence because God is silence, stillness, peace and calm: that which is the being of all that is, the potentiality of everything, and therefore no thing in particular. We do not talk to God; God does not talk to us – at least not in any literal sense. This is why it is important to realize that contemplative prayer is not about talking to God so much as listening to the voice of silence in our hearts. And we cannot possibly be listening if we are too busy doing all the talking.

Being truly silent is easier said than done, of course, and if we try to be silent we will soon discover just how unruly and chaotic the mind really is. Yet this is where we need to focus our efforts, for it is only 'in secret' that we are likely to encounter the God 'who is in secret'. If we pray to God in secret then, says Jesus, God who 'sees in secret' will reward us. This suggests, first, that to enter the presence of God, to be seen by God, is its own reward and, second, that since God sees what is hidden, or secret, he knows who we really are and what we really need.[11] Moreover, seeing 'in secret', God acts in secret. In other words, we do not always know about the influence of God in our lives. We do not always know if and when our prayers are answered. We do not know how many miracles are occurring every day and all around us.

Similarly, we may think nothing is happening as a result of our efforts to pray and meditate. We may be tempted to wonder

---

8 Psalm 46.10
9 Psalm 62.1, 5; Cf. 37.7
10 Zephaniah 1.7; Cf. Habakkuk 2.20
11 Matthew 6.8

why we bother, as we seem not to be making any progress. But if God rewards us in secret, then it follows that we will be rewarded in ways we may not expect and of which we may not even be aware. In his letter to the Romans, Paul writes that 'the Spirit helps us in our weakness; for we do not know how to pray as we ought, but that very Spirit intercedes with sighs too deep for words'.[12] For all we know, our lives and the world around us are being transformed daily as a result of our practice without us even realizing it. After all, the fruits of prayer seldom occur during the time of prayer itself, such as in the form of 'experiences', but afterwards, perhaps even years later. Indeed, it is often when our practice seems to be at its most boring, fruitless and unproductive, when we seem to be making little or no progress at all, that the greatest transformation is occurring. This is precisely why our prayer life needs to be built on the foundation of a solid discipline, so that we persevere with it even when we think we are getting nowhere. And it all starts with going into a room.

Obstructions

I will never forget the first time I attended a meditation class. I arrived full of eager anticipation. For many years I had been fascinated by the spiritual traditions of Asia, and was yearning to go beyond merely reading books about meditation: it was time to learn how to do it. When the class began, however, we were all just told – with no further explanation – to start meditating. I had expected some sort of guidance, but there was none. As the dimly lit room fell silent, I started to feel intensely self-conscious, not sure what I was meant to be doing, or thinking about. I assumed from the lack of instruction that the others present were all seasoned experts. I shifted about uneasily, trying to get comfortable, or simply because I had no idea what else to do. The teacher noticed this and told me to keep still. That at least gave me something to focus on.

12 Romans 8.26

Many spiritual traditions claim that stillness of body leads to stillness of mind, and that being still – both physically and mentally – is necessary if we are to be fully present to the reality that is what is. Sitting still and calming the mind are closely related. We will find it much easier to draw the mind back from its restless wanderings if we are able to keep ourselves physically still. But while it can be hard enough to sit still for any length of time – especially if we are not used to it – keeping the mind still is almost impossible. Our media-saturated lives are so bombarded with sensory stimulation, and we have become so addicted to it, that we probably do not even realize how distracted we are most of the time, and how seldom we are truly present. Do we really give our full and undivided attention to the things we do, or the people we are with? Being present is not as easy as it might sound. Ultimately it implies accepting what is as it is, and ourselves as we are, without wishing things could be otherwise, or imagining that if only they were, then everything would be just right. Paradoxically, being present also requires a certain amount of distance. If we wish to be present to the presence of God – or even one another – we will need to be slightly detached from the controlling influence of our fluctuating and manipulative moods and feelings. We will need to take a step back from ourselves in order to see what is really going on.

One of the first things we discover when we take up meditation is that it is almost impossible to silence the ceaseless chatter of the mind. Instead of the blissful calm we may have hoped we would experience, we are more likely to find ourselves being swept away by a torrent of random and often unexpected thoughts, leaving us anywhere and everywhere but present to the here and now. If the mind is left with nothing in particular to think about then a spate of memories, fantasies and obsessive thoughts soon flood in to fill the void. The same often happens when people go on retreat, and are forced to give up many of the activities with which they normally fill their lives. And it is what happens to Jesus in the well-known story of the 'temptation in the wilderness', a story taken by the first Christian contemplatives as the model for their spiritual practice.

Following his baptism by John, Jesus is moved by the Spirit to withdraw into the wilderness, where he remains for 40 days and 40 nights. During this time he is approached by Satan, who tries to tempt him with thoughts of gluttony, avarice and vanity in order to distract him from his purpose and ensnare him in webs of deceit, fantasy and delusion.[13] It is interesting to note Mark's characteristic use of the word 'immediately' in his brief account of this episode. It seems to suggest that as soon as we take up a spiritual or ascetic practice – as soon as we put our hand to the plough of the spiritual life, to borrow another gospel metaphor – we can *immediately* expect to be confronted by obstacles.[14] In the Parable of the Sower, Jesus describes how in the spiritual life – and this is especially true of when we are trying to meditate – we are frequently led astray, easily put off after the first flush of enthusiasm, and distracted by our desires and cares.[15] These obstructions, which, of course, for the most part come from within us, were characterized in the early Christian contemplative tradition as demons. After all, the Greek word, *diabolos* – from which we get the word devil – literally means something like 'to throw across'. Thus demons are the stumbling blocks we encounter in the spiritual life, the obstructions that are 'thrown across' our path.[16] They are whatever comes between us and that which is God.

In the days of the early Church, Christian ascetics were inspired to follow the example of Jesus by going into the desert in order to seek God. They did this, not because God can only be found in the wilderness, but because it is arguably easier to abide in the presence of God when there is less to distract us from being focused on God alone. Living in the desert they experienced the same sort of temptations as Jesus, and in due course they classified the various hindrances they encountered into different categories of obsessive thoughts or 'demons'.

---

13 Matthew 4.1–11; Mark 1.12–13; Luke 4.1–13
14 Luke 9.62
15 Mathew 13.18–23; Mark 4.14–20; Luke 8.11–15
16 Matthew 16.23; 1 Thessalonians 2.18

Reading this literature today, one gets the unmistakable impression that they personified as demons experiences that we would be more likely to articulate in psychological terms. Describing the activity of demons was their way of analysing certain aspects of human behaviour, in order to gain a greater understanding not only of themselves, but also the God in whose image we are made. The object of the spiritual practice they developed was to become aware of these 'demons', to see how and when they were at work in the mind, and then to resist or counteract their attempts to 'possess' them. From the gospel narratives we can surmise that Jesus had the self-awareness to know, straight away, what the devil was up to, and so he was able to dispatch the distracting thought immediately, by citing a verse from scripture to act as a counter-thought to negate the devil's sly insinuations. We are unlikely to be as successful, yet we face exactly the same task: to try to become aware of what is really going on in our thoughts and behaviour, to understand ourselves more fully, and thereby the ground of our being as well. This process became known as the 'discernment of spirits', but we might simply call it mindfulness. It is essentially the self-awareness that we strive to cultivate through meditation.

The 'temptation in the wilderness' thus became the prototype for all Christian asceticism. From the accounts we have we can infer that the principal obstructions in the spiritual life invariably involve gluttony, avarice and vanity; and that the best way to resist these 'demons' is with fasting, charity and prayer. According to the story, Jesus has been living in the wilderness and fasting for six weeks. Knowing he is absolutely famished, the devil makes his first move as the demon of gluttony in order to tempt him with his hunger, saying, 'If you are the Son of God, command these stones to become loaves of bread.' Jesus replies, quoting the Law of Moses in Deuteronomy, 'One does not live by bread alone, but by every word that comes from the mouth of God.'[17] The point he is making, of course, is that in order to be most fully human we need not

---

17 Matthew 4.3–4 (Deuteronomy 8.13); Cf. Luke 4.3–4

only physical sustenance, but also spiritual nourishment. Gluttony therefore has a wider meaning here, in the context of an ascetic discipline, than we usually accord it in ordinary everyday usage. It is not so much a matter of excessive greed and self-indulgence, but rather the tendency to obsess about our physical needs – which is exactly what we do when our appetites are restricted. Anyone who has tried to go on a diet will be very well acquainted with this particular demon. Ironically, we live today in a society of excessive consumption and profligate waste that is at the same time obsessed with health and fitness, dieting and bodily image. The consumer society is in thrall to the demon of gluttony, the personification of craving itself. Gluttony in all its many guises dominates our contemporary narratives of identity construction: we are what we consume.

Gluttony is opposed by fasting, which, whether understood in the narrow sense of simply not eating, or more widely in terms of restraining our consumption, is probably the most common form of ascetic discipline. It is certainly one of the simplest, being something that almost anyone can do, whatever their situation in life. No surprise then that giving up something we are in the habit of eating – or perhaps drinking – is so common during Lent, the traditional season of abstinence in the Christian year. Some people become vegetarian, others give up alcohol, and many forego chocolate. Although it may be hard to see how not eating chocolate for six weeks is really going to result in deep and lasting inner transformation – especially since we are likely to gorge ourselves on it come Easter Sunday – sincerely undertaken, giving up something we habitually consume can be a very useful discipline. Just as gluttony is not simply about eating too much, so fasting is not merely about eating less, but rather a symbol of restraint and moderation regarding our patterns of consumption generally. To give something up is to force a change in our lifestyle and this inevitably draws our attention towards it, prompting us to examine our behaviour more closely. Sacrificing our physical hunger in order to nourish our spiritual hunger can thus be a very useful aid in the cultivation of self-awareness.

Matthew and Luke both describe the same three temptations, but list them in a different order. Following the sequence in Luke, the second of the temptations is avarice. The devil offers Jesus all the power and wealth in the world, boastfully claiming that it has been given to him to give to whomever he pleases.[18] Indeed, looking at some aspects of modern life, it does not seem too far-fetched to suggest that the devil really is the lord of this world: after all, the demon of avarice is clearly hard at work in contemporary society.[19] Jesus responds by asserting that God alone is worthy of our praise, implying that avarice, which entails the creation of some object of desire, is thus tantamount to idolatry. Unfortunately, avarice is almost invincible – especially, it would seem, when manifested in the form of an all-consuming consumerism. Even attempts to subvert the consumerist agenda are inexorably subsumed into its totalitarian narrative and re-packaged for our compliant consumption.

The demon of avarice strikes whenever we seek satisfaction in the acquisition of some worldly good, whether concrete or abstract. It is thus present in our identification with all the things we possess – and not just things, but our achievements and personal qualities as well. Avarice feeds on the mistaken belief that we actually own things when, of course, ultimately we do not. Not until we learn to give up the illusion of being the owner of things, the things we think we possess but which in reality possess us, can we really begin to tackle this profoundly corrosive obstruction. And this requires careful and honest observation of our own minds and behaviour. One of the most subtle but deadly manifestations of the demon of avarice is the temptation to seek perfection in our spiritual practice, to imagine that there is a final goal to be attained, in which all will be resolved. To focus on achieving 'success' in this way can only lead to further frustration and disappointment when we inevitably fail to reach the desired state of perfection.

18 Luke 4.5–8 (Deuteronomy 6.13); Cf. Matthew 4.8–10
19 2 Corinthians 4.4

Finally, the devil tempts Jesus to reveal his power over life and death by throwing himself off the pinnacle of the temple in Jerusalem and invoking the angels to save him. This is a manifestation of the demon of vanity, as the devil is here trying to entice Jesus to prove that he really is the Son of God. Jesus, of course, refuses, declaring that we should not be so presumptuous as to think we can put God to the test.[20] Unfortunately for us, however, since we do not have the fully realized self-awareness of Christ, the demon of vanity can be all but irresistible. It is in many ways the fundamental sin, stoking the egocentrism that lies at the root of so many expressions of our unenlightened and often damaging behaviour. It can be found at work in the common, and in some circumstances understandable, tendency to seek affirmation in the praise and admiration of other people. It dictates how we present ourselves to the world, and it is the driving force behind a great many of our motivations. Indeed, this demon is so subtle and devious that it can even appear disguised as a spiritual virtue, snaring us when we imagine we are doing good deeds, such as when we help others and receive the reward of their appreciation, or the soothing of our conscience. Vanity hides in the false humility to which many fall prey in spiritual life. And it accompanies all the other temptations, waiting to step into the breach when one of them is defeated, thus giving the demons further opportunity to attack. This is why it is so difficult to resist or overcome this particular demon, as any success we may have against it can all too easily become another source of vanity. The only remedy is the genuine and deep humility that undergirds an attitude of sincere prayer.

Jesus refuses to be snared by the devil's insidious mind games. In fact, he does not allow the conversation to develop at all, but each time quickly cuts it short with a sharp retort that silences the unwelcome intrusion. The lesson here for us is that temptation cannot be avoided – not even Jesus was immune – but it can be evaded. Unfortunately, like all these things, preventing

---

20 Luke 4.9–12 (Deuteronomy 6.16); Matthew 4.5–7

ourselves from being lured in by this train of thought or that mental conversation is easier said than done. One only need meditate for a short time to realize that thoughts just come and go of their own accord, and there is nothing we can do to stop them: thinking is simply what the mind does. But although we may have no control over whether demons, or thoughts, come into our mind, we do at least have some say in whether or not they take up residence.

Resistance is not futile, but it is far from easy. Demons are by nature deceptive, which is why it is so fiendishly difficult to understand the behaviour of the mind – especially our own. But if we can try to see the subtle ways in which the demons of gluttony, avarice and vanity are at work in our lives then – by becoming aware of these tendencies in ourselves – we can take a first step towards being free of their controlling influence. In order to do that, we need to notice when they manifest in our thoughts and actions. We need to watch ourselves closely, observing our thoughts without getting caught up in them, and then as soon as we see what is going on, if a demon is at work in us, as it were, then we must cast it out. And believe me, that is the easy bit; it is spotting them in the first place that is tricky.

Describing aspects of human psychology in terms of the activity of demons may seem a little unusual to modern sensibilities, but it was commonplace in the ancient world. The Bible contains a great profusion of evil spirits and, on the evidence of the gospels, Jesus seems to have spent a good deal of his time exorcizing them.[21] The trouble is, however, we can find it difficult these days to take such stories seriously. Generally speaking we do not think of the world as being inhabited by spirits or supernatural forces. As a result, most people will either dismiss these narratives as pure fantasy, or else try to re-interpret them in ways that are more consistent with a modern scientific worldview, such as in terms of psychiatric conditions.

---

21 Matthew 8.16, 32; 9.33; 12.22; 17.18; Mark 1.34, 39; 5.13; 7.29; 19.9; Luke 4.35; 8.2, 33; 9.42; 11.14; 13.32

It is hard to tell, from our perspective, whether people in ancient times actually thought that demons were real or 'merely' a psychological metaphor. No doubt many did have what we would now call a literal view of things, but, having said that, so do many in our own time. Either way, it is interesting to note the use of the Greek term *logismoi* when referring to demons in the literature of early Christian monasticism. *Logismoi* can be translated as 'obsessive thought', and it should be easy enough for us to see how the influence and effect of obsessive thoughts might be equated with the more graphic language of demonic possession. In everyday conversation we can refer to someone as 'having a demon', and we also have a tendency to 'demonize' those whom we find it hard to accept or relate to. We commonly talk about the 'demon drink' – which can cause people to act in ways that are literally subhuman – or about people being so consumed by powerful feelings, such as jealousy, that they act 'like one possessed'. Indeed, we are all familiar with the way in which strong passions – anger would be a good example – can sometimes and quite literally possess a person, to the extent that they actually become the emotion in question. When someone is angry we do not say they are 'feeling angry', but that they *are* angry. It is total. And the same is true for the other obsessive thoughts or emotions by which we may be consumed and possessed.

We should be wary, however, of jumping to the conclusion that demons are 'nothing but' thoughts, or of trying to draw too sharp a distinction between modern concepts of literal truth and metaphorical interpretation. Overly reductive attempts to 'demythologize' the supernatural betray a failure to recognize the very real power of the imagination to shape the world as we experience it. When Jesus says that the one who looks with lust has already committed adultery in their heart, he is testifying to the fact that the imagination can have a very powerful impact on reality.[22] There is nothing unreal about the very tangible and often destructive effects that obsessive thoughts can sometimes

22 Matthew 5.28

have, which makes it all the more interesting to consider these ancient discourses for their astute and closely observed reading of the human mind and its behaviour. Obsessive thoughts can develop a life of their own: they can consume us, and literally occupy or possess us. I am able to think of numerous occasions when my mind was possessed by an obsessive thought that I could not control, and which in fact ended up controlling me, often to my detriment. Demons afflict us all the time. This is why it is so important that we not only learn to see and understand how obsessive thoughts work, but also try to free ourselves from their power and dominion.

The obsessive thoughts characterized above as demons are the obstacles that come between us and the truth of things we call God; they manifest as the behaviour patterns that we identify as our personality. This personality is not our true self, of course, but rather a mask projected by the ego, a constructed self, comprising a whole host of demons – or personality characteristics – such as vanity, greed, anger and pride. These constructs of the self are the evil spirits that Jesus was so frequently called upon to exorcize. And yet, surprisingly, when he did so, the reaction of bystanders could sometimes be rather less than positive. When he heals the man possessed by a legion of demons in the country of the Gerasenes, dramatically casting the evil spirits out of the man and into a herd of pigs who run over the edge of a cliff, the people ask Jesus to go away, because 'they were seized with a great fear'.[23] But why should they be afraid when they see people being healed? Surely they should be pleased?

There could be a number of things going on here. Perhaps they were afraid because Jesus appears to have a power that makes him different to them; a power, moreover, that they cannot understand. And then they might start to wonder. How is it that he has command over evil spirits? Maybe it is because he is in league with them?[24] Or it could be a subconscious fear

---

23 Luke 8.37; Cf. Mark 5.15; Matthew 8.34
24 Matthew 12.24; Mark 3.22; Luke 11.15

that they are not even able to articulate. If these 'evil spirits' are our delusions – the false personalities that have become us, and which we unwittingly continue to feed and nurture – then having them driven out would indeed feel deeply threatening. If Jesus is the truth, and – as the icon of God – the true self of all, then the false self is bound to feel intimidated, whether aware of the reason for it or not. We are all, in various ways, 'possessed': by our fears, our hopes, our dreams and delusions – not to mention our material possessions and habits of consumption. If we are to follow the path of wholeness and holiness represented by Jesus, who points towards the divine truth in us all, then the demons of our false selves, with which we mistakenly identify, which deceive us into thinking they are real, must be cast out.

No wonder people were afraid of him.

Attention

The demons we have been talking about do not just cause our restlessness of spirit; they are the very spirit of restlessness and agitation itself. Resisting the demons and stilling the mind are two ways of describing the same thing. This is why the first task in meditation is to learn how to be still, mentally as well as physically. There are various ways in which we can try to do this, but all of them in some way involve keeping our attention focused on a single object – shutting the door, as it were, to other thoughts – until the mind settles down and becomes tranquil and un-distracted. There is a passage in Matthew's Gospel, which in the King James Version reads, 'The light of the body is the eye: if therefore thine eye be single, thy whole body shall be full of light.'[25] In other words, if we are focused and single-minded, looking only towards the one thing that really matters, then the whole of our being will be purified, or 'full of light'. Modern translations usually render this phrase: 'if your eye is

---

25 Matthew 6.22; Cf. Luke 11.34

healthy'. Although in this case the Authorised Version actually provides the more literal translation of the original Greek, the notion of 'healthy eyes' also makes a good deal of sense here. Singleness of mind helps us to see things the way they really are. To see things as they really are is to see with 'healthy' eyes.

The idea that seeing things the way they really are involves healthy, sound or 'single-eyed' awareness also helps to explain why meditation is sometimes described in terms of purifying the heart, the organ traditionally understood as being the seat of the mind. In the Christian tradition, the notion of purity of heart derives from the teachings of Jesus in the Sermon on the Mount. 'Blessed are the pure in heart, for they will see God.'[26] One who is 'pure in heart' is not only a paragon of virtues, such as kindness and honesty, but also free from delusion and falsehood, wholly focused on and given to that which is God. If we would see God as he is, we need to purify ourselves, and refine the way we see things, so that we become pure, as he is pure.[27] Purity, in this sense, is not simply a matter of being morally untainted: it is about being tried 'like gold in the furnace'.[28] Seen in these terms, meditation is the process of burning away all the impurity, the mental constructs or institutions of the self – the thoughts, feelings, demons and delusions – that stand between us and God. By such means we come to see, with 'unveiled faces . . . the glory of the Lord as if reflected in a mirror' and are thereby 'transformed into the same image from one degree of glory to another'.[29]

The practice of meditation, or purifying the heart, typically involves some method of keeping our attention anchored, such as by focusing it on a single object, in order to draw the mind back from its ceaseless wanderings and hold it steady. Popular techniques include the use of mantras or prayer words, visualizations and icons, or mindfulness of breathing. The remainder

---

26 Matthew 5.8
27 1 John 3.2–3
28 Wisdom 3.6
29 2 Corinthians 3.18

of this chapter will consider the use of the breath as a focus for meditation as this is widely recognized to be one of the simplest and most effective ways of calming the mind and cultivating stillness. Concentration on the breath is often also combined with the recitation of a prayer word or mantra, in such a way that the repetition of the word or prayer is synchronized with the breathing. Arguably the most common form of meditation, variations on this basic method can be found in almost all trad-itions, including Christianity. For example, Paul's injunction to pray without ceasing is usually given as the inspiration for the Orthodox practice of reciting the Jesus Prayer in time with the breathing.[30]

The use of the breath as the focus for meditation has much to commend it. Our breathing is always present: it is one of our automatic physiological processes and yet, at the same time, it is also an activity that we can to some extent control – unlike our heartbeat or the workings of our liver and kidneys. We can regulate our breathing at will, making it fast or slow, shallow or deep. We can even hold our breath for short periods and stop breathing altogether. Not that we should try to breathe in any particular way when we meditate. On the contrary, our breathing should be relaxed and natural, as this will have a calming effect on the mind. The breath thus functions as a link between body and mind, a bridge enabling us to cross from agi-tation and distraction to calm awareness of the here and now. This can easily be demonstrated from our ordinary everyday experience. Our breathing naturally slows down when we con-centrate on an intricate task, whereas if we are frightened or anxious, it becomes shallow and quick – which is why we com-monly take a deep breath when we need to calm ourselves.

Because the breath represents this profound connection between the spiritual and material dimensions of our being, it tends to be associated with potent symbolism. In the Genesis story, when God creates Adam and Eve, he breathes the breath

---

30 1 Thessalonians 5.17

of life into them – hence our concept of a soul or spirit.[31] The notion that our breath represents life itself, and that it comes from God, is assumed to be a self-evident truth throughout the literature of the Old Testament. For example, one of the characters in the book of Job declares, 'The spirit of God has made me, and the breath of the Almighty gives me life.'[32] And in the New Testament, Jesus echoes the act of creation, breathing on his disciples and saying, 'Receive the Holy Spirit.'[33] According to the Bible, therefore, the breath we breathe is the breath of God, and the animating spirit of life within us. Indeed, the breath is one of our vital signs, indicating that we are alive. But the insubstantiality of the breath also alerts us to the fragile contingency of existence. We are but 'a mere breath', says the Psalmist, on more than one occasion.[34] Life is as ephemeral as a puff of air: 'the dust returns to the earth as it was, and the breath returns to God who gave it'.[35] Yet, at the same time, our breath is also what we have in common with that which is the source of all that is.[36] Therefore, if the breath symbolizes the intimate connection between creature and creator, then perhaps through it we can somehow re-connect with God.

Thinking about the breath in this way also helps us to realize that, just as our breath is always with us, so in our spiritual practice, we do not have to go anywhere or achieve anything; we just have to be. We do not have to follow a special programme or master a complicated technique; we just have to wake up to the reality of who and what we really are, and abide in the fundamental intuition of being that is what is. In deep meditation we may cease to be aware of ourselves as separate, individual beings, as we realize instead that we are but part of the ultimate reality that is being itself. It is sometimes

---

31 Genesis 2.7
32 Job 33.4; Cf. 7.7, 16; 12.10; 32.8; Psalm 33.6; Ecclesiastes 12.7
33 John 20.22
34 Psalm 39.5, 11; Cf. 62.9; 78.33; 94.11; 104.29; 144.4; 146.4
35 Ecclesiastes 12.7
36 Isaiah 42.5

thought that contemplative prayer or meditation is self-centred, but in fact the opposite is true. In communion with God, whose breath animates all that lives, we become one with the whole of existence.

God may be present everywhere – the life of what lives, the existence of what exists – but we will never come to know this if we are too preoccupied with ourselves and caught up in the busyness of our lives. The only place we can meet God is here, and the only time is now. Being in the here and now means keeping the mind still. It means being quiet enough to hear the whispering of the spirit. As we strip away our constructs of the self, and delve ever deeper into the reality of the present moment, we are left eventually not with nothing, but the pure awareness that is what is: an experience of existence at its most essential. This fundamental intuition of being makes us present to the presence of God. For if we are made in the image and likeness of God, if God is the word we use to describe the reality that is what is, then the most basic level of our being – being itself – must somehow be related to that which is God. In deep meditation we thus 'become participants in the divine nature'.[37]

---

37 2 Peter 1.4

6

The Murmuring Mind

As they journeyed through the desert, the Israelites were constantly grumbling and complaining – against God, and against
their leaders Moses and Aaron.[1] 'Why have you brought us up
out of Egypt to die in the wilderness?' they moaned. 'For there
is no food and no water, and we detest this miserable food.'[2]

How little human nature has changed during the intervening
millennia! We can probably even empathize with them: to this
day the kind of food available when travelling often leaves a
little to be desired. But their complaint reveals more than just a
feeling of being out of sorts. First of all, the Israelites are here
succumbing to the common delusion of imagining the past as
being better than it actually was, which is something we tend
to do whenever the vicissitudes of life make the present seem
unpalatable. Second, they are consumed with anxiety about
food and bodily comfort. 'We remember the fish we used to eat
in Egypt for nothing,' they wail, 'the cucumbers, the melons,
the leeks, the onions, and the garlic.'[3] Their obsessive thoughts
about melons and cucumbers are as clear an indication as any
that they are being harassed by the demon of gluttony, which,
as we saw in the previous chapter, always comes calling at the
first hint of privation. Nostalgic yearning for a supposedly
better past – or utopian delusions of a perfect future, for that
matter – together with an obsessive preoccupation with bodily

---

1 Exodus 15.24; 16.2; 17.3; Numbers 11.1; 14.2–3, 27, 29, 36;
Joshua 9.18; Psalm 106.25
2 Numbers 21.5
3 Numbers 11.5

gratification, represent some of the archetypal distractions we are likely to encounter when we embark upon a spiritual path.

Meditation leads us on a testing journey through a mental wilderness, plagued with the demons of our thoughts, where we will be confronted by the same trials and tribulations that were faced by the Israelites as they roamed the trackless wastes of the desert. We will grumble and complain bitterly – if only to ourselves – and we will rebel against the discipline we have undertaken. Any excuse will be enough to put us off. Obstacles will throw themselves across our path; distractions will steal our attention and lead us astray. These will include both the disturbances that come from within, namely our thoughts, as well as all the sounds and activity we perceive in the world around us. Sometimes, we might find these external distractions to be so off-putting that we cannot even begin to concentrate. But if we pay close attention to what is really going on in our mind, we will see that the true source of the disturbance is not the sound or activity outside, but our reaction to it, the irritation we experience on account of it, and the noise of our internal commentary on it. Even external distractions can thus be reduced to our thoughts. If we wish to overcome distraction, we need to let go of the thought of being distracted. This is not as hard as it may at first seem. With a little practice we can learn to see that the things we blame for diverting our attention are, like us, simply part of the reality that is what is – the here and now to which we are endeavouring to be present – rather than an interruption of it or something separate from us. Understood in these terms, we may find it easier to accept the background noise of the world as just that: background noise, and nothing for us to react against or be concerned about. Once we realize that what we call 'distractions' are really our own reactions projected onto the blank canvas of reality as it is in itself, they will cease to be distracting.

This tendency to indulge in our internal commentary, on the world and the people around us, is known in the Bible as 'murmuring'. We see evidence of murmuring coursing through the story of the Israelites in the wilderness like a stain on the relationship between humanity and God. We encounter murmuring in the Gospels too, such as when the crowds – in particular the Scribes and the Pharisees – mutter and complain about Jesus.[4] And in his first letter to the Corinthians, Paul reflects on the destructive effects of murmuring with reference to the experience of the Israelites in the desert.[5] Indeed, murmuring seems to be a particular affliction of faith communities, as anyone in a position of ministry or religious leadership will no doubt be able to testify.

Murmuring is essentially the unconscious habit we have of comparing others unfavourably with ourselves. It manifests as comment and criticism, gossip, chitchat, backstabbing and snide remarks. Just to be clear, murmuring is not the expression of a legitimate complaint, or even the voicing of a grievance or disagreement. It is something altogether more iniquitous, which very often includes the attribution of our own faults to others. Murmuring is the corrosive, poisonous whispering that prevents us from being open and listening to each other, and – worst of all – it is something that we all do, all the time. Murmuring occurs not only when we are explicitly grumbling aloud about everything that is wrong with the world; it is also present in our thoughts. We are murmuring when we mentally criticize or find fault with people. We are murmuring whenever we note how things would be so much better if only they were done my way. Indeed, if we listen carefully to our internal commentary, we will find that we are murmuring almost continuously. Left unchecked, murmuring can easily become an all-pervasive critical attitude to everything, which entrenches us in ruts of negativity and sours our relationships – with the world, with other people, with God and within ourselves. In the Letter of James, the tongue is described as 'a restless evil, full of deadly poison'.[6] This is not putting things too strongly. The incessant bickering and complaining of the Israelites in the

---

4 Luke 5.30; 15.2; 19.7; John 6.41, 43, 61; 7.12, 32
5 1 Corinthians 10.10; Cf. James 5.9
6 James 3.6–10

wilderness actually caused Moses to become ill and lose his strength.[7] It will make us ill too. Murmuring really can be that destructive.

Unfortunately, murmuring comes so naturally to us that most of the time we are not even aware that we are doing it – let alone how poisonous and destructive it can be. It is so much a part of normal life, an expression of the ordinary activity of the mind, that it becomes something like a mental wallpaper, or background music, which we only notice if it is not there. If we make an effort to be aware of it, however, we are likely to find ourselves murmuring in our everyday conversation, as we complain about things or make judgemental comments about others. We will also notice ourselves murmuring in our thoughts and, most of all, we will find ourselves murmuring when we are trying to meditate. When we catch ourselves murmuring in meditation, we should simply acknowledge the thought for what it is and let it go. But our discipline of mindfulness is not only to be applied during those special times we set aside for being quiet. We need to become aware of our murmuring at all times, mindful of our thoughts and words – and our impact on others – so that our meditation practice extends into the whole of life.

The problem is, however, that we are for the most part so absorbed in our self-centred preoccupations and so caught up in our internal commentary on life – in other words, murmuring – that we are very rarely present to the reality in front of us or the people around us. How can we be truly listening to life if there is a voice in our heads that is already doing all the talking, distracting us from the here and now, and preventing us from being present – to ourselves, to each other and ultimately to God? How can we expect to see what is really going on if we are unable to see beyond the narrow confines of our own personal perspective? How do we imagine we will be able to connect with others if the projections of our ego keep getting in the way? Taken to the extreme, murmuring can become such

---

7 Numbers 11.14; Psalm 106.32

an obstacle to open and honest interaction between people that it contaminates the life of a community, undermines the fundamental relationships that sustain it, and eventually destroys it altogether. This is exactly what happened to the Israelites in the desert. In response to their incessant murmuring, God sent deadly, venomous snakes.[8] Murmuring literally ended up poisoning them.

But then something rather interesting happens. Moses makes a serpent of bronze and puts it on a pole. Anyone who had been bitten by the snakes – or poisoned by the malignant demons of their egotism – was to look at the bronze serpent and, as a result of what strikes me as being something like a homeopathic remedy, they would be saved from death.[9] The rationale of homeopathic medicine is based on the idea that a disease can be treated with a small quantity of something that would produce the same symptoms in a healthy person. Leaving aside the question of whether such claims withstand empirical testing, anyone who has treated a hangover by consuming more alcohol – the so-called hair of the dog – will have an intuitive grasp of the basic principle. Similarly, in terms of our inner life, sometimes just seeing the problem, the cause of the 'poison' as it were, is enough to free ourselves from its power. This notion of what we might call 'spiritual homeopathy' could provide another perspective on not only the 'lifting up' of the bronze serpent, but also the crucifixion of Jesus, whose physical death brings spiritual life, and which, according to John, the episode of the bronze serpent prefigures.[10]

The mysterious and paradoxical truth revealed in the death of Jesus on the cross – that through suffering there is ultimately an end to suffering – can thus be seen as a kind of 'homeopathic' remedy for spiritual disease. By the shocking sin of nailing the Son of God to a tree, sin itself is redeemed. Brought low, he was raised up. In defeat he was victorious.

---

8 Numbers 21.6
9 Numbers 21.9
10 John 3.14

Through death comes new life. In giving up the 'I', emptying the self of itself – as Jesus did on the cross – the self is truly fulfilled.[11] The sign of the cross represents an 'I' crossed out: following the self-emptying way of Christ leads not to our obliteration – we will not perish, but have eternal life – for by giving up our false selves we come into the perfect fullness of being that is God.[12]

This apparently simple – but in reality very difficult message – is repeated again and again throughout the New Testament. Jesus clearly says that those who would be his disciples must lose their life in order to find it.[13] In other words, to be most fully who and what we really are, we have to give ourselves up; we have to surrender the constructs of the self that stand between us and our neighbour, and ultimately God. It is these constructs of the self that we hear murmuring inside our heads.

Thoughts

Meditation is about holding the mind in a delicate balance, and not – as is often, but wrongly, supposed – an attempt to stop the mind from thinking. Indeed, it should not take us too long to realize that this is impossible. Nothing stimulates thoughts like trying not to think; and the moment we become aware that we are not thinking, we have had another thought. The truth is we can no more stop thinking than we can stop breathing, a fact that further emphasizes the link between the breath and the mind. Indeed, our thoughts are 'but an empty breath'.[14] Insubstantial. Ephemeral. And, like the breath, ever present.

---

11 Philippians 2.7
12 John 3.15
13 Matthew 16.24–5, 10.39; Mark 8.34–5; Luke 9.23–44, 17.33; Cf. John 12.25
14 Psalm 94.11

Most people probably do not spend a lot of time thinking about thoughts. We do not tend to ask ourselves what our thoughts are. Perhaps we think it a silly question. Thoughts are thoughts: they are what we think. But, of course, this is no explanation at all. We may think we know what thoughts are, but in fact if we spend a bit of time watching them, we may be surprised by what we see. For a start, thoughts can sometimes have a life of their own. They can be out of control, and they can end up controlling us. They can even – odd as this might sound – drive us out of our mind. It is important, therefore, that we have some understanding of what exactly it is that we are talking about when we talk about our thoughts.

If we look carefully, we will discover that any thought can be broken down into bits of basic information, ultimately derived from our sense impressions. This is because everything we experience through the senses, in every moment of consciousness, is recorded as a simple unit of mental data. These bits of raw data are then combined and compounded to produce the complex mental phenomena we call thoughts – in much the same way that individual words can be arranged in an infinite number of different configurations to produce an infinite variety of sentences and paragraphs. All the thoughts, feelings and ideas we have – including abstract concepts – can thus be reduced to combinations and permutations of primary information, derived from our sense experiences. As we meditate, sitting quietly and observing the constant manipulation of this mental data, we can dissolve each thought into its rudimentary components and simply let them go, like leaves blown by the wind.

Initially we may suppose that we have lots of different kinds of thoughts, but I suggest they can all be reduced to just two fundamental categories. All our mental activity, in all its apparent variety, can be seen to consist either of reliving the past (which has ceased to exist) or speculating about the future (which has yet to exist). In other words, we have only two narrative genres: history and fantasy, vehicles respectively of memory and hope. All our thoughts can be classified as one or other

97

of these two types, and then dismissed as being irrelevant to the present moment.[15] After all, neither the past nor the future presently exist, so if we are caught up in our thoughts then we cannot be in the here and now, which means we cannot be present to God, the world, each other, or even ourselves. If we are caught up in our thoughts we are not abiding in the awareness of reality as it is, but floating instead in a fantasy world we have constructed and projected onto the simple truth of what is. Admittedly it is both natural and necessary to situate ourselves in the context of a past and in relation to a future, even if neither are presently real. Indeed, the assumption that we will still exist in the future gives meaning to what we do in the present; if we were not able to make that assumption, everyday life would be impossible. So it takes a certain amount of courage to let that go and simply allow ourselves to abide in the indeterminate present, as it is, rather than as we think we want it to be. The cultivation of self-awareness is, therefore, neither more nor less than an exercise in deconstructing our projections and letting go of our sense of identification with our thoughts and all that comes between us and the way things are. Ultimately it means letting go of the idea of 'me' that is most obviously manifested as the ceaseless chatter of our inner voice.

Thoughts come and go of their own accord, whether we want them to or not. We may imagine that the mind is a systematic processor of information, rather like a computer, and that we are in control of its operations, but this is clearly not the case. When we are not consciously thinking about something in particular, the mind does not just stop thinking: it becomes a swirling kaleidoscopic flux of random churning images, thoughts, memories and fantasies. Scenes unfold before the mind's eye as if we are watching a film. We cannot arrest this dream-like stream of consciousness, because that is just the mind being what it is and doing what it does. Moreover, if we try to control or suppress it, this will only reinforce the mistaken notion

---

15 Matthew 6.34; Cf. 1 Timothy 6.8

that we are the 'owner' of the thoughts that we are, in meditation, trying to let go.

When we meditate we will find ourselves thinking about all
sorts of things. Most of the time our attention will be completely swept away by our thoughts, and we will be lucky if
we manage to experience even brief moments of respite from
the constant flow. It is not the purpose of meditation to try
to suppress this activity, however, but to see it for what it is,
because – as is so often the case – seeing it is the first, and often
most important, step. Before we can wake up, we have to realize that we are dreaming. If we are able to take a step back
from ourselves and our habitual sense of identification with
our thoughts – which come and go regardless of whether we
are consciously 'thinking' – then we may be able to see ourselves as the observer of our thoughts, rather than the thinker
of them. This is similar to the experience of being half-asleep
and half-awake at the same time, when the mind is starting to
dream, but we are still partly aware of what is going on around
us. In this state of semi-consciousness, we can separate the idea
of the thinker from the process of thinking.

Just as staring at an object till our eyes go out of focus will
loosen the sense of connection between seer, seeing, and the
thing seen, so in meditation our thoughts drift out of focus
when we anchor our attention to a single point of awareness,
such as our breathing or prayer word. Not that we stop thinking, of course, but we may stop being the thinker, even if only
for a moment. When we meditate we try to become a passive
witness of – rather than participant in – our thoughts, watching them as they arise of their own accord, before gently letting them go, without getting personally involved, or allowing
ourselves to slip into the starring role of our mental movie.
An element of discipline is thus essential to the cultivation of
awareness, but it requires both a conscious effort and a light
touch. Any attempt to resist thoughts only leads to more thinking. Meditation is not about the absence of thoughts, but a
particular kind of detachment from them, a letting go that is
achieved by keeping our attention anchored to a single object.

This calls for a delicate balancing act, like being both relaxed and alert at the same time. On the one hand, if we try too hard, we are imposing our will, the 'I' gets in the way and we will not reach the pure awareness that only arises when we are making no effort. On the other hand, a degree of conscious intention is necessary in order to keep our attention poised so that it does not stray from the here and now and wander aimlessly in memory and fantasy. So we must let go with a very gentle and effortless effort of the mind, in order to avoid being snared in either of the two traps of trying to suppress our thoughts, on the one hand, or carelessly identifying with them on the other.

As we become aware of each thought, and see how it is stealing our attention away from the present moment, we can decide to label it – either as memory or fantasy, and therefore irrelevant – and then just gently let it go. Naming our thoughts in this way can neutralize their grip and make it easier for us to pick up the thought, as it were, and drop it into an imaginary bin, rather like deleting a file on a computer. Maintaining the presence of mind to label and let go of each thought as it arises, without being pulled in by it, is no mean feat. It is almost impossible to remain in such a refined state of awareness for more than a few moments at a time. But that is okay. Whenever our attention drifts away and gets captured by another thought, as it will again and again, we just have to keep coming back to our point of focus, be that the breath, mantra or both. If we are able to do this every time that we realize our mind has strayed, we will eventually slow the constant stream of thoughts and discover the peaceful gap that lies between them. Though we cannot stop the mind from thinking, we can lengthen the gap between our thoughts, just as when we hold our breath we lengthen the gap between breaths.

Letting go of thoughts as they arise requires constant vigilance and a certain degree of disciplined awareness. Most of the time our attention will be swept away by the unstoppable flow of mental activity. As you try to observe, as if from afar, the thoughts coming and going like clouds floating on the breeze, try not to get involved, try not to get carried away by them, try not to allow yourself to become the subject or thinker of those thoughts. Try to see them for what they are. Try to see that what we ordinarily think of as 'our thoughts' are not really 'our' thoughts at all, because they come and go as they please, whether we are thinking them or not. Try to see this, and try to see that everything we think is either a recollection of something that has already occurred, and therefore no longer exists, or a speculation regarding a future that has not yet come about, and may never actually happen. If, as the thoughts arise, you are able to identify them as memory or fantasy, and therefore not relevant to the present moment, then it may become easier to let go of the illusion of being the thinker, caught up in the drama of that mental movie in which we imagine ourselves in the starring role.

The practice of meditation involves a conscious intention to keep gently returning our attention to the present moment. With sustained practice, this should lead to deeper and deeper levels of stillness, which in turn will allow self-awareness to blossom. Of course, there may be times when the mind will not be still, however diligently we apply ourselves, because we are preoccupied with something distressing or important. While it is true that most of what goes through our mind when trying to meditate may be of little significance, sometimes there are thoughts we cannot relinquish, and on some occasions that is because they really do require our attention. Surely we should not be trying to ignore them? Surely the fact that something so insistently demands our attention is an indication that we need to deal with it? There is no doubt that if we are very angry, upset or anxious, it will be impossible to meditate. In such circumstances, we need not worry or feel guilty about it: sometimes we simply cannot meditate, and that is fine. Although, having said that, it could also be true that making the effort to meditate is just what we need most in that moment.

The Psalms, as ever, offer pertinent counsel. 'When you are disturbed, do not sin; ponder it on your beds and be silent.'[16] It

---

16 Psalm 4.4

may be that sticking to our discipline and creating some mental space through meditation will allow things to work themselves out, or clear a mental blockage, and lead to a resolution we were otherwise unable to achieve. After all, meditation is not about trying to stop the mind from thinking, but just quietly observing the endless procession of random thoughts, without getting personally involved in them. If we do find that we are able to resolve some knotty problem in meditation, it will be precisely because our discipline has enabled us to take a step back from ourselves and put things into perspective, allowing a solution to emerge into view.

Perseverance

The Israelites found the wilderness hard and punishing. Our own spiritual journey may be the same. Like them, we may at times find ourselves being led astray or tempted to give up. Perseverance, then, is a crucial component of any spiritual practice – without it we cannot hope to get far – so it should come as no surprise to discover that stories of perseverance abound in biblical literature. For example, in the Book of Genesis there is a story about Jacob wrestling with a strange man, sometimes said to have been an angel. Because he refuses to give up, he is renamed Israel, 'the one who strives with God'.[17] By perseverance he becomes who he is really meant to be. In the second of his letters to Timothy, Paul exhorts him to 'endure suffering'.[18] And in Luke's Gospel, we hear Jesus telling his disciples a story about a widow who doggedly persists with her legal claim until the judge finally grants her petition.[19] Perseverance is one of the strongest expressions of faith: faith that the journey has a worthwhile destination, in spite of how things may sometimes seem. Unless we 'run with perseverance the race that is

17 Genesis 32.22–30
18 2 Timothy 4.5
19 Luke 18.1–8

set before us' – whether that be a task, a journey or a relationship – we cannot hope for a fruitful outcome.[20]

This should alert us to the fact that, far from being an idle self-indulgence or an easy ride, the spiritual life presents us with a very demanding challenge. Yet, we may still be forgiven for wondering why, if it is all about just 'being ourselves', it has to be such hard work. While it is certainly true that to meditate is to abide in the deepest reality of what we are, the problem is we have lost sight of this 'true self', lying hidden beneath all the layers of our constructed personalities. And, moreover, just as we would not expect to understand all there is to know about quantum physics after a single lesson, or to lose weight after a single workout, so we should not expect to know everything about the spiritual life after a single meditation class. It is a process that takes time, sometimes a whole lifetime. We all know that we can never hope to achieve anything in life unless we stick at it, whether this is learning a new skill, going on a diet or getting fit. We have to commit to the discipline. Spirituality, unfortunately, is the same. The first time Moses received the Law on Mount Sinai, he dropped the tablets and it was lost. Then the Law was given a second time.[21] This can happen often enough in life generally, and the spiritual life is no exception. We fall down; we get up again – and again, and again.

The necessity of perseverance should be obvious enough, yet we are fickle creatures, on the whole, with a tendency to blame external circumstances when, more often than not, the problem is as likely to be our own unwillingness to take responsibility for ourselves. I constantly allow myself to be put off by the slightest inconvenience, or to get side-tracked by what might appear to be more attractive options. Most people will no doubt be familiar with the experience of thinking that the grass is greener on the other side of the fence, even though we know it never is. When the going got tough, the Israelites were all too easily distracted and seduced: by false gods, false

20 Hebrews 12.1
21 Exodus 34

memories and false hopes. As they grew more and more fed up with the hardships of their journey, they lost faith in God and in Moses and decided to construct and worship an idol instead – the Golden Calf – wrongly imagining that this would appease or even satisfy their frustrated desires.[22]

We do exactly the same thing whenever we slip into a fantasy about how our lives will be complete, if only certain circumstances could be changed in order to make things just the way we want them to be. All our desires have the potential to become idols, which is why the story of the Golden Calf is such a potent symbol for the multitude of distractions that may beset us along the way. It is hardly surprising that the Ten Commandments place such a strong emphasis on injunctions against idolatry. Idolatry is making something a god that is not God – it is to substitute a mere image for the thing itself – and as the Psalm says, 'those who make them are like them', that is, lifeless.[23] Worshipping gods other than the one true God is deemed to be the greatest sin of all: it leads to spiritual death.

Idolatry lurks not only in the distractions that can arise from hardship and privation, but also in the distractions of prosperity and comfort. The Book of Deuteronomy describes how the Israelites became idolaters as soon as they gained a degree of material wealth and security.[24] As then, so now: once our basic needs are satisfied, we forget our dependence on God, imagining instead that we are masters of our own destiny, and that our good fortune has come about as the result of the work of our own hands. Idolatry is, in many ways, the defining mark of the individualistic consumer society. It pervades the utopian delusions and discourses of modern culture like a virus, which is why Paul's advice to the Colossians is as relevant today as it must have been in his own time. 'Set your mind on things

---

22 Exodus 32
23 Psalm 115.8; Cf. 97.7
24 Deuteronomy 8.11–20

that are above, not on things that are on earth,' he says, before clearly identifying idolatry with greed.[25]

In his correspondence with Timothy, Paul paints a vivid picture of the decadent self-indulgence, egotism and vanity of his world and ours in terms of the 'last days' when 'distressing times will come'. He then goes on to describe these times in which people will be 'lovers of themselves, lovers of money, boasters, arrogant, abusive, disobedient to their parents, ungrateful, unholy, inhuman, implacable, slanderers, profligates, brutes, haters of good, treacherous, reckless, swollen with conceit, lovers of pleasure rather than lovers of God'.[26] These are signs of the times, applicable not only to the world in which Paul and Timothy lived, but our own as well. Indeed, we are always living in the 'end times'. When Paul talks about the 'last days', the final age to which he refers is the end of faith – whether in society or the individual – that is inevitably characterized as a time when people become lovers of pleasure, that is, of themselves, rather than God. Now, as in Paul's day, we love nothing but self and money. Now, as in Paul's day, we are ruled by gods of our own making. Now, as in Paul's day, 'people will not put up with sound doctrine, but having itching ears, they will accumulate for themselves teachers to suit their own desires, and will turn away from listening to the truth and wander away to myths'.[27]

Given the ubiquitous culture of individualism and consumerism in which – like it or not – we are all steeped, it is no wonder that many people seem to think that perseverance, remaining stable and rooted, implies a rigid stubbornness that is repressive and can only lead to stagnation. But perseverance has nothing to do with stagnation or stifling creativity. Rather, it is to stand firm and be persistent. Perseverance is precisely what enables us to rise to the challenges presented by life's inevitable changes. It implies engaging fully with the situation at

---

25 Colossians 3.2, 5; Cf. Romans 1.24–5
26 2 Timothy 3.1–4; Cf. Wisdom 2.6–9
27 2 Timothy 4.3–4

hand, and remaining steadfast in the face of obstacles, in spite of what might initially appear to be more appealing prospects. This is not the same as being fatalistic. The situation in which we find ourselves may, as was the case with Jacob, require us to contend against it. Nevertheless, in order to engage more effectively, whatever the circumstances, we have to understand that the challenges we face may be an opportunity for growth. Failing to take responsibility by blaming others or constantly flitting from one thing to the next will be more likely to increase our frustration than resolve it. Growth, by contrast, comes from persevering through adversity. Perseverance enables us to overcome our conditioning and become who and what we really are.

In spite of the times when life – or just our meditation practice, for that matter – seems bleak or even hopeless, it is perseverance, rather than giving up when we cannot be bothered to make the effort, that gets us through. 'Be persistent,' says Paul, 'whether the time is favourable or unfavourable.'[28] Perseverance enables us to create those positive habits that help sustain us on the journey. Unfortunately, however, we are often unwilling to do more than the minimum required to achieve immediate results, not realizing that sometimes it is necessary to make a sacrifice in the present for the sake of a greater reward in the future. Jesus introduces his story about the widow and the unjust judge as a parable about the need 'to pray always and not to lose heart'.[29] Perseverance is thus an essential part of faith. It takes trust to make a commitment for the sake of an outcome that cannot be known in advance. We should be able to see something of the truth of this in our own everyday experience. Mastering a skill, establishing a career, or even just getting to know somebody, are ordinary examples of things that cannot and do not just happen instantly, but take time – perhaps even a whole lifetime – and only come to fruition as the result of sustained commitment.

---

28 2 Timothy 4.2
29 Luke 18.1

Like any discipline, meditation requires time and effort. And, as we have seen, the wilderness within is fraught with obstacles and distractions. If we manage to stick at it, however, we may in time cultivate sufficient mindfulness to maintain our focus and avoid being led astray – at least for a few moments. Thoughts will not cease as long as there is breath in the body, but their constant flow might slow down a little. If and when this happens, we may experience a gap opening up between them. This inner space is truly silent, truly empty. In its stillness it is timeless, because time implies movement. Abiding in this gap, free from all the noise and clutter with which we normally fill our minds, we may experience an awareness of the still centre behind the surface activity of our conscious mind. We may find that we have stopped repeating our mantra. We may even stop breathing for a few seconds, without realizing it, forgetting for a moment our physical discomfort, or indeed that we are a body at all. We may have the feeling that we are unlimited consciousness, pure essence of reality. In this still, silent, empty space at the heart of being itself, we may become open to the possibility of an encounter with what is; we may find ourselves present to the presence of that which is God. Although, of course, as soon as we realize it, we have had another thought . . .

Being present to God comes at a price, however, for it means being open to scrutiny and the attendant risk of being transformed from who we think we are into who God knows us to be. If God is truly God, he must see everything we do, and know everything that resides in our hearts.[30] If we were really to live as if we truly believed this, it would be profoundly life-changing. I would never do or say half the things I do if I really believed it was all seen and recorded, and that I would be held to account for my words and deeds at the end of the day. This is why sticking at it is the necessary foundation for spiritual growth: it implies taking responsibility for our actions – and their consequences – and thereby acknowledging a truth of

---

30 Psalm 139.2–4, 94.11, 44.21; Cf. Matthew 6.8

things greater than that which we simply decide for ourselves. Through perseverance, especially when the going gets tough, we – like Jacob – encounter God, the deepest reality of what we are, and are transformed by that encounter, becoming, as a result, more than what we were. Jacob emerged from his struggle as a new person. 'You shall no longer be called Jacob', said the stranger, 'but Israel, for you have striven with God and with humans, and have prevailed.'[31] It is through the very struggle with God that Jacob becomes who he is really meant to be.

---

31 Genesis 32.28

7

Standing on Holy Ground

To meditate is to abide in that fundamental intuition of being that is the deepest reality of what we are. But it requires a profound stillness of mind truly to be present, here and now, to reality as it really is. As soon as we start to meditate, we will discover that most of our time is actually spent elsewhere, anywhere but the present. We will find ourselves thinking about all the things we would rather be doing, the pressing tasks we know await our attention, the people we need to see, the things we want to say to them, and so on. We will be having conversations in our head, playing out fantasy scenarios of future events, or re-running episodes from our past, perhaps imagining how some encounter or other could have turned out differently if only we had said such and such. Indeed, as we have already noted, all our thoughts can be reduced to recollections of the past or speculations about the future: both arguably futile and pointless exercises, and sure signs of a distracted and unfocused mind. If we are caught up in our thoughts, we are clearly not in a state of quietness. It should not take us too long to realize that it is easier to talk about being silent than it is to achieve it. But if we persevere in our efforts to be still, we should notice the incessant chatter of our mind subside a little – or become easier to ignore – and the gaps between our thoughts lengthen sufficiently to allow for the silent empty heart of being itself to open up within us.

Silence

People often tell me they find silence disturbing, and they may well have good reasons for feeling that way. In some circumstances silence can have very negative connotations. We talk about victims of oppression being silenced or not having a voice – although, to be fair, this is not usually what people have in mind when they say they find silence disturbing in the context of meditation. Here it is more to do with the fact that we are so addicted to entertainment, and the stimulation it provides, that its absence seems abnormal. As a result we may feel anxious, unnerved or a little exposed. And so whenever we find ourselves in a quiet situation, we immediately want to compensate by filling it with noise. Some of us do this more than others, but perhaps we all do it to a greater or lesser extent. We do it when we are with people and when we are alone. We do it when we automatically switch on the television or radio, even though we are not really watching or listening to anything in particular, or when we play music just for the sake of having something on in the background. And anyone who travels on public transport can hardly fail to notice all the people plugged into headphones, or fiddling with their smartphones. If we are constantly besieged by noise, we will never experience the beauty of silence. Indeed, it would seem that many of us choose deliberately to avoid it. No wonder we dread the so-called 'awkward silence' that descends like fog when people run out of things to say to each other. No wonder we find it hard to break a silence, becoming increasingly uncomfortable as we desperately try to think of something to say. But why should silence be awkward? Why do we feel it necessary to break it, to shun silence at all costs, even if it means talking rubbish, or filling the air with noise in order to keep silence at bay? Why do we find it so difficult to cope with being alone or silent? Why do we seem to think that silence is somehow unnatural?

The notion of breaking a silence suggests not that silence is unnatural, but rather that it is something whole. According to the biblical creation story, in the beginning the world was 'a formless void'.[1] If there was nothing, there was nothing to make a noise: there would have been silence. And from the infinite potentiality that is nothing and everything at the same time, creation emerges. God breaks the first awkward silence with his creative word and in so doing calls the world as we know it into being. 'By the word of the Lord the heavens were made, and all their host by the breath of his mouth,' says the Psalmist, 'For he spoke and it came to be.'[2] If the world as we know it – the intelligible world of human experience – is a world created and ordered by the word of God, by language, then it follows that to know silence is to know the underlying reality beneath that, the clay from which all pots are made, reality as it really is.

What is true of the world is true also of our personalities, constructed as they are by and from language. All the various phenomena with which we identify as I, me, and mine – our memories, opinions, thoughts and feelings – are narrative forms, mediated by language, articulated in words. As silence discloses the nature of reality as it is in itself, so in the same way our basic nature is revealed to have the essential characteristic of silence. By comparison what we call our personality is but a cacophony of noisy thoughts. In common with all thoughts, our different constructs of the self come and go, like clouds on the wind, without enduring substance. As we meditate, sitting quietly and observing our stream of consciousness, we may feel that behind it there is no thinker; indeed, we will see that the 'thinker' is just another thought. When we stop doing all the things we do to occupy our lives and minds, and allow ourselves to be still and silent, we may also become aware of a profound emptiness, and feel acutely conscious of the fact that our busy lives often lack real content. When the things with which we habitually fill that emptiness are taken away – such

---

1 Genesis 1.2
2 Psalm 33.6, 9

as the pursuits, variously, of pleasure and power – we are left staring into the primordial void at the heart of being.

The temptation is to fill this void with something – an idol, effectively – of our own making or imagining. But rather than doing that we could try instead to see that what we initially experience as a disquieting emptiness is in reality the joyous fullness of being itself. It only appears to us as 'emptiness' because the pure and undifferentiated totality of what is, being everything, is not any one thing in particular, thus offering nothing for us to latch onto and identify with as I, me or mine. In order to see this, to know the reality of being, hidden behind the self that has been created out of all our thoughts, memories and desires, we have to be silent. Only by silencing the clamour of the ego, manifested as all our various mental constructions, and withdrawing our attention from the things that consume and possess us, may we come to know the ground of our being as it is in itself. Self-knowledge is also, therefore, a kind of self-forgetting, a process of unknowing. Thus, self-awareness grows in direct proportion to the diminishing of our ego, as we let go of our sense of identification with the legion of falsehoods from which we have constructed ourselves and instead quietly abide in the simple intuition of being that is what is.

To be silent – truly silent – is to dissolve all the projections that make up the story that we call 'me' and 'my life'. To be silent is to be present: not floating in fantasy or memory, not thinking of this or that. It is to see things as they are, rather than as we think we would like them to be. By spending a little time in silence, we will really notice how most of the time we are simply not present, not even to ourselves or each other – never mind God – because we are living instead in the past or the future. We can only encounter God – or truth if you prefer that word – in the silent emptiness of being that is the deepest reality of what we are, the place where, emptied of our constructed selves, we can abide in that in which 'we live and move and have our being'.[3] Silence is the necessary pre-requisite for

---

3 Acts 17.28

knowledge of the self, and also therefore knowledge of the God in whose image we are made. Not that we are God, of course, but we are, ultimately, what God is.

There is a lot we can say about silence. Ironically, it is much easier to talk about silence than actually to be silent. Yet it is essential to our spiritual and general well-being sometimes to take time out, to be quiet for a bit, and give ourselves a chance to see things as they are. Normally speaking, we do not see things the way they really are, but the way we are: that is, re-created in the image of our own desires. Silence allows us to put a little distance between ourselves and all the projections and obsessions that, quite literally, occupy our lives, our time, and our minds. To be silent, therefore, is to put things into perspective and cultivate the detachment we need in order to be more truly connected. It is to let go of our needless preoccupation with the past and the future, and become aware instead of the still centre behind our internal commentary, allowing in turn for the possibility of an encounter with God, or the reality that is what is.

People are often surprised when they discover that Christianity has a tradition of contemplative spirituality. We are more used to associating this sort of thing with Eastern religions. But the truth is, contemplation lies at the heart of the Christian tradition and, moreover, silent prayer has an impeccable pedigree. After all, Jesus was in the habit of withdrawing to deserted places, often spending the night in prayer on the mountainside, or getting up early and disappearing off by himself to be alone with God.[4] He was also in the habit of maintaining silence when to speak would have been to speak in error, such as when he was asked to judge the woman caught in adultery and when Pilate challenged him to defend himself against his accusers.[5] As well as advising us not to 'heap up empty phrases', like the hypocrites who 'think that they will be heard because of

---

4 Mark 1.35, 6.46; Matthew 14.23, 26.36; Luke 5.16, 6.12, 9.18, 22.41; John 6.15

5 John 8.6; Mark 15.5

their many words', Jesus commands us to 'pray in secret'.[6] A secret is something – assumed to be true – about which we keep silent, telling no one. This subtle correspondence between truth and silence can also be noted whenever Jesus reveals his divine nature. For example, in Mark's Gospel he heals a leper, a deaf man, and the daughter of Jarius, in each case charging those concerned not to say anything to anyone.[7] They must keep silence. When he casts out demons, he commands them to be silent – that is, to cease to be – for their very nature is confusing, distracting chatter.[8] When Peter confesses that Jesus is the Messiah, Jesus instructs the other disciples not to tell anyone about it.[9] And at the time of his Transfiguration, those who are with him have an experience of God in the cloud, which renders them speechless.[10]

It is perhaps most common to think about the Transfiguration in visual terms. There is a shining light, a change in appearance. It is a very visual story, the record of an event seen, a revelation beheld by the eyes. But in an interesting detail, Luke ends his account of the incident by saying, 'The disciples kept silence and, at that time, told no one what they had seen.'[11] Is that not rather odd? Surely their first instinct would have been to go and tell everyone what an unusual thing they had witnessed. But instead, they were silent.

They were silent because silence is our natural reaction to something awe-inspiring, like a glorious view or a magnificent work of art. Most people will be familiar with the experience of being stunned into silence by an experience that beggars belief. If God is that which words cannot circumscribe, then silence really is the only appropriate response to an encounter with the divine.[12] Silence and revelation thus go hand in hand: if an

---

6 Matthew 6.6–7
7 Mark 1.44, 7.36, 5.43
8 Mark 1.25, 34; Cf. Luke 4.35, 41
9 Mark 8.29–30; Cf. Matthew 16.20
10 Mark 9.9; Luke 9.36; Matthew 17.9
11 Luke 9.36
12 Zechariah 2.13

encounter with God leads to silence, then perhaps silence – or putting ourselves to one side – can lead to an encounter with God. This is the basic rationale behind the practice of contemplative prayer. After all, words are inadequate to the task of describing God; language reaches its limit when confronted by the unlimited. If there is nothing we can say about God, then we must be silent if we would be present to the presence of God. The cultivation of silence is the necessary precondition for understanding this most unfathomable truth. True knowledge of God is predicated on silence.[13] True knowledge of God requires us to undergo a profound unknowing of everything that is not God.

God

People argue endlessly about God. Whether or not he exists; whether or not he is almighty; whether or not he loves us. But these questions are, very often, a misleading distraction. The answer to the question of God's existence depends on what we mean by God in the first place, and the problem here is that our ideas about God are the greatest obstacle to actual knowledge of God. If, with many of the people who do not believe in God, it is thought that the word refers to some sort of super-human being – or indeed any kind of entity that somehow exists as an object in the world out there – then I have to confess I do not believe in God either.

But if God is understood as a word that refers to the ground of being – the deepest reality of what we are and the irreducible fact of consciousness – then to deny the existence of God is, perversely, to deny the existence of existence itself. When we talk about the existence of God we are not talking about whether or not God 'exists' in the same way as when we talk about the existence of other objects in the world, because God is not among those classes of things. This means, of course,

---

13 Psalm 46.10; 62.1, 5

that I do not – and indeed cannot – *know* whether God 'exists', or is real and true. But I can and do know that there is 'something' to which the word God refers; and that, whether God is really 'real' or not, there is a reality and a truth that we name when we use the word 'God'. So it is not really a question of 'does God exist?' as if we are debating the existence of some particular 'thing' among other things, but rather that by definition, God refers to what ultimately exists, the bottom line if you like. That is simply what the word 'God' means. God is not something that exists, but existence itself; or to be more precise, the necessary and sufficient condition for the existence of existence, as we know it, manifested here and now. Likewise, it is not so much a question of whether or not God is true, but rather that God is the word we use when we want to talk about truth itself.

God is that which is beyond, in the sense of representing the point or purpose of things beyond the immediate fact of their basic actuality, as well as in the sense that God is beyond limitation and beyond understanding. God is the word we utter in response to the profound silence of unknowing with regard to ultimate truth. God is absolute transcendence, and yet also intimate, immediate and immanent. God is being itself: not a being, but the totality of being. God is that which is, the will to be, consciousness knowing itself manifested as 'other'. God is the Good, whatever that might be. God is the Truth, whatever that might mean. God is the giver of life, and life itself: the very breath you draw, the drawing of the very breath you draw. And, above all, God is love: the fundamental creative energy of all that is.[14] This, in turn, reveals the profound truth that reality is ultimately purposive and intentional, that 'what is' is meant to be. To acknowledge God is to affirm that the core of our being is grounded in rational and relational consciousness. When we talk about God we are not talking about something 'out there', but rather, we are saying something about the irreducible fact of existence. Our existence.

---

14 1 John 4.8, 12, 16

In Christianity there is a stream of what is known as 'negative' or 'apophatic' theology. This denotes a way of talking about God that emphasizes what we do not know and cannot say, an acknowledgment of the fact that anything we say about God is inevitably and ultimately going to be untrue. In his letter to the Romans, Paul talks about God's 'inscrutable' ways, before paraphrasing a line from Isaiah's lofty paean to the majestic transcendence of God.[15] The Psalms, too, hint at the profound 'darkness' of God, whose knowledge is 'too wonderful for me . . . so high that I cannot attain it'.[16] The discipline of meditation is thus the means by which we not only take a step back from the noise that fills the mind, but we also let go of the words with which we construct our world. In meditation, we gradually refine, purify – and finally give up – all our concepts of God. We reach the truth by shaking off what is false, like Moses taking off his shoes in order to approach God in the burning bush.[17] Our shoes are what we stand in; they symbolize our understanding, our conceptual knowledge: the views, images and opinions that come between us and reality as it is in itself, the ground of being, the ground on which we stand. Moses stood before God in his bare feet, his footprints representing his true identity rather than the constructed identity projected by his shoes. Standing on holy ground, he had to remove his humanly constructed understanding of things as they appear in ordinary everyday life in order truly to understand things as they really are in terms of God, or that which is ultimately real and ultimately true.

The deepest reality of what we are is the ground of being we all share. There is in a sense, therefore, no need to seek God, for God is the 'holy ground' upon which we all stand. We do not need to search for God, but rather we need to let God find us. In the same way, we should not view the practice of meditation as being somehow separate from everyday life,

---

15 Romans 11.33–34; Cf. Isaiah 40.13–14
16 Psalm 139.6, 92.5; Cf. Isaiah 55.9; Job 21.22
17 Exodus 3.5

but here and now, in every sense. God is already with us, and not somewhere or something far removed from us. This is why it is sometimes said that if we want to know God then first we must know ourselves. At the same time, we only come to know ourselves by knowing others, for the self is a reflection of other people. And the ultimate 'other', of course, is God, who is other than all that we know and all that we ordinarily are. This is also why the paradoxical result of going deeper into the self is that we draw closer to others, for that which is most personal is also that which is most universal.

As Moses stands before God in the burning bush, he asks for a name. God answers, 'I am who I am.'[18] I can imagine Moses doing a double-take and thinking, "What kind of a name is that?" But this is very much the point: it is a way of saying that God has no name, because God is such that 'he' cannot be named. God is not an object in the world, to be classified and bound by our definitions, like all the other things to which – following Adam – we give names.[19] To name something is to distinguish it in relation to other things. But God is absolute, not relative; God is being itself, not a being that can be reduced to a concept, or an entity that can be differentiated from other entities. The word 'God' does not have a 'meaning' in the same way that other words do, for it is the word we use to denote the horizon of meaning itself, the foundational assumption upon which the rest of thought is constructed. How could God have a name as we do? God is what is. God is simply 'I am'. This is why there is ultimately nothing we can say about what God is, only that God is. What is just is; it is both everything and, at the same time, nothing in particular.

The burning bush, it is often noted, burns while remaining unconsumed by the flames.[20] In other words, the fire is self-sustaining: it needs no fuel. It is, like God, self-caused, requiring no foundation. Thus the burning bush symbolizes the

---

18 Exodus 3.14
19 Genesis 2.19–20
20 Exodus 3.2

simple fact of being, the sheer mystery of existence itself, the fundamental irreducibility of consciousness: that which simply is. God in the burning bush is formless, causeless, not of this world, with a name that is no name. All our concepts of God are inadequate, because such concepts are an attempt to reduce the totality of being to something we can understand, and God is – by definition – that which the human mind cannot understand. Even Moses, who talked freely with God, was still not permitted to see him face to face – that is, to know him intimately – 'for no one shall see me and live'.[21] The most we can know about God is that God is profoundly unknowable.

Doubt

If God cannot be known in any ordinary sense, does that not make it rather difficult – if not impossible – for us to believe in him? It is hardly surprising that people have trouble making the proverbial leap of faith. Interestingly, although we may assume that religious scepticism is a relatively modern phenomenon, even the disciples of Jesus could have their faith called into question. Judas betrayed him, Peter denied him, and Thomas – like so many today – doubted him. I have always been able to identify with 'Doubting Thomas'. He is – without doubt – my favourite disciple. Like us, he is sceptical and unsure of things. He doubts. He is a very modern kind of disciple too: somewhat literal-minded, demanding empirical proof. 'I'll believe it if I see it,' is basically what he says.[22] And, more often than not, we do exactly the same. Indeed it is almost universally taken for granted that proof of the sort you can see and touch is the only kind that counts – even though we know perfectly well that things are not always what they seem, and also that there

---

21 Exodus 33.20
22 John 20.19–29

are many other ways in which things can be verified. Seeing is not believing, after all.[23]

Yet such is the way we have come to think about the world that even though we know appearances can be deceptive, it is simply taken for granted that empirical proof is the measure of all truth. This assumption is fundamental to our modern scientific worldview, and that worldview is often held to be at odds with a religious worldview. Not, as some might think, because one is true and the other false, but precisely because both are true, albeit in different ways. Unfortunately, however, we make the mistake of judging one in the light of the other – as if they were of a kind – and so end up talking at cross purposes.

The failure to grasp this important point causes much of the misunderstanding that characterizes the tired debate between science and religion. There is no good reason why one cannot subscribe to both a scientific account of how the world works and a religious account of the meaning and value of human existence. Science pertains to what we think we know about the world. It represents the current state of human knowledge. It is not so much a collection of facts as a method for working things out. Religion is about what we believe to be the meaning of human existence. It too is not about facts, so much as our relationship to questions of ultimate concern. Therefore, we do not have to choose between science and religion, or discard one in favour of the other. Both are relevant and necessary to human flourishing. Both, in their own way, are vehicles of truth. But they are also incommensurable: you cannot reduce one to the other. Describing a smile in terms of the activity of the muscles in the face will tell you nothing about what it means – or what we experience – when someone smiles at us. Similarly, we may describe a painting either in terms of the chemical composition of the pigments used in making it, or in terms of what it represents. Both types of description are complete in themselves and perfectly true, but neither tells us everything there is to know.

---

23 Matthew 21.32

Moreover, you cannot translate from one to the other, reduce one to the other, or combine them meaningfully in the same sentence. You cannot, for example, describe a painting of the Madonna and Child as a picture of the Virgin Mary holding a patch of canvas daubed in flesh tones.

Yet, we often seem to forget that different things can be true in different ways. Truths about human experience expressed in poetry or metaphor, scientific facts about the natural world, and moral truths of good conduct are all true by virtue of the relevant criteria. This is why it is absurd to imagine that one can prove or disprove the existence of God as if it were a scientific hypothesis that could be verified empirically. A god that could be proven scientifically – that is, comprehended by human reason – would not be God but an idol, an image of our own making. Faith is not an assertion akin to a scientific proposition, but a choice we make in favour of a particular attitude to life, on the understanding that doing so is conducive to human flourishing and personal fulfilment. It is not a matter of making dogmatic statements about the world, so much as living our life as if God was real. Indeed, it requires a degree of agnosticism regarding ultimate truth in order to live as if the story is true in the meantime. Faith – by its very nature – is concerned with those things about which we do not and cannot have certain knowledge, such as the purpose of human existence, the meaning of suffering and how to live the good life. It is not about having solutions to insoluble problems, but the means by which we live with ambiguity and paradox. The trouble is, of course, that in the face of uncertainty, we yearn for some sort of security – the security and confidence of certain knowledge – and sometimes we may be tempted to express our faith in ways that imply such certainty. Sometimes people can seem very sure of their convictions about matters of which nobody could possibly be certain. Ironically, this yearning for security may actually prevent genuine faith from arising.

The opposite of faith is commonly supposed to be doubt, but nothing could be further from the truth. Faith and doubt are mutually dependent, not mutually exclusive: you cannot have one without the other. Doubt is not the opposite of faith but – like Thomas – its twin. The opposite of doubt would be certainty, and certainty leaves no room for faith. Faith must therefore entail at least the possibility of doubt; otherwise it would not be faith. If I knew all the answers, I would not need faith – or trust or hope – because I would simply know. Faith is not, therefore, anything to do with what we imagine to be knowledge – quite the opposite in fact. It is concerned with that which we do not – indeed cannot – know. There is at the heart of human existence an irreducible mystery. Who are we? Why are we here? What is it all about, finally? 'Faith' is what gives us the means to live with that mystery, trusting that in spite of all appearances to the contrary, there is a meaning and a point to it after all. Faith is not a set of answers to put an end to all questioning, but a decision to carry on exploring the mystery of being human. Faith is what enables us to live with the questions that cannot be answered. It is about trust and it is about hope. And this is the lesson that Thomas, like so many of us today, needs to learn.

Faith would be unsustainable, however, if it were a merely private decision, if we just made a personal choice to subscribe to a particular opinion about things. And this is the other great lesson of the Thomas story. For faith to be justified – that is, for us to be able to trust in something amid all the uncertainty of life – it needs to be something that is shared and thus validated by being held in common with others. It is the shared community of faith, and the mutual accountability this implies, that makes faith real. We are all in it together. To have faith is to belong to a group of people who collectively inhabit a story in which human life, in its otherwise baffling complexity and incomprehensible absurdity, is made to make sense. Our spirituality might be personal, but it can never be private. Belief in God, or any notion of a 'higher' truth, entails certain duties and obligations. As the Bible makes clear, we have responsibilities to each other – for our collective security and well-being – chief among these being the commandment to love our neighbours as ourselves.[24]

This challenges the view, widely held by both believers and atheists alike, that faith is all about a belief system, that our religious identity is defined by adherence to a list of doctrinal propositions. This is completely back to front. We may intuitively think that beliefs come first, and that a way of life or practice derives from them, but in fact, it is more often the other way around. The way of life comes first, and then we rationalize and justify it in retrospect. Faith is seldom something you work out in your head by weighing up the pros and cons and coming to a fully formed conclusion. It is far more often a way of being in the world that matures gradually over time, and does so most naturally as the result of participation in a faith community. Faith is almost invariably acquired from the example of others, from family and friends, and only very rarely the outcome of an isolated cognitive process. It is, in short, something you do, and not simply – as widely supposed – something you think.

We can easily see the truth of this by asking whether it is more important to do good deeds or to think good thoughts. It may be assumed that we need to have right beliefs in order to do right actions, but this is simply not true. It is perfectly possible to profess all the right beliefs and commit all the wrong actions, or – conversely – to live a godly and virtuous life, while knowing absolutely nothing about the finer points of theology. This is the implication of the story Jesus tells about the two sons sent to work in the vineyard.[25] The first says he will not go, but then changes his mind and goes; the second says he will go, but does nothing of the sort. 'Which of the two', asks Jesus, 'did the will of his father?' Clearly, it was the first. Talk is cheap: it is what you do that counts. Now, of course, this is not to say it does not matter what you believe in. Far from it. But what matters just as much, and often more, is what you do about it. The point being

24 Leviticus 19.12–18; Cf. John 13.34
25 Matthew 21.28–30

that our beliefs are private and, in themselves, without consequence, whereas our actions are public and invariably have an
impact on others and the world around us.

This notion that faith is primarily about a way of life
rather than a set of beliefs finds cogent expression in the Letter of James. 'Be doers of the word and not merely hearers,'
he writes.[26] 'What good is it, my brothers and sisters, if you
say you have faith but do not have works?'[27] In other words,
what is the use of saying all the right things, if the beliefs we
profess are not reflected in how we act in the world? It is on
account of a discrepancy between their words and their deeds
that religious people and authorities are so often accused of
hypocrisy, and sometimes not without justification. The point,
as James puts it, is that 'faith by itself, if it has no works,
is dead'.[28] This is because a faith that has no outworking in
action remains hidden – it may as well not exist – whereas
actions demonstrate the faith that lies behind them.[29] Even the
demons, he adds, believe in God; it is through their actions
that they reveal their true nature. The essence of faith, according to James, is not mere adherence to this or that doctrine,
but a commitment to right action: 'to care for orphans and
widows in their distress, and to keep oneself unstained by
the world'.[30] We may wish to re-formulate our specific social
or pastoral priorities, depending on context, but the point is
clear: what matters is living a virtuous life. Without that, our
faith, our spirituality and our high-minded sentiments are all
in vain.

When we participate in a common practice we act as one,
we become a unity – like a crowd at a sporting fixture – even
though within that unity there will undoubtedly be differing
views and opinions about all sorts of things. Common practices,

26 James 1.22
27 James 2.14
28 James 2.17
29 James 2.18
30 James 1.27

more than shared beliefs, define a community and give it an identity that is recognizable to others. This is why, when it comes to religious faith, doing what we do is at least as significant as saying what we say. In some ways, it may even be more significant. Seeing faith in terms of practice, as a way of life rather than a set of beliefs or propositions, thus serves at least two useful purposes relevant to our topic. First, it may help persuade the person of faith that the practice of meditation is not a peripheral add-on to their core beliefs, or a speciality for religious professionals. Meditation is the practice of the spiritual life: it belongs at the heart of anybody's faith. Second, it may encourage the person who practises meditation, but who rejects the idea of being part of a faith community, to see that the practice of the spiritual life cannot be a solely private enterprise. Our faith – whether explicitly religious or not – is that which binds us in networks of responsibility and accountability for and to each other, thereby serving to relate us more comprehensively to the narrative of our common humanity.

Faith is not a matter of signing up to a set of beliefs and propositions, so much as belonging to a community that shares a particular attitude to life and way of being in the world. This is why it is quite incoherent to suppose – as many evidently do these days – that you can be a Christian without going to church or, for that matter, spiritual but not religious. Participation in the shared story of a worldview and its way of life needs to come before we can expect to understand the truths expressed in doctrines. Belonging must come before believing and not, as some would have it, the other way around. You have to do it before and in order to understand why; and this too is the point of the Thomas story. He was not present in the house with the rest of the disciples the first time Jesus appeared to them, meaning that in a sense he did not belong; so how could he believe? The next time Jesus appears among them, Thomas is present. It is not so much that he had to see in order to believe, but that he had to be there – he had to do it – in order to understand. The same is true for us.

Conclusion

Mary And Martha

When I made the life-changing decision to follow the spiritual path, wherever it might lead me, I immediately found myself caught between two conflicting calls: withdrawal from the world on the one hand, and engagement with the world on the other. I felt a strong urge to explore the possibility of joining a monastery, and I also felt, equally strongly, that there were numerous 'worldly' aspirations I still needed to fulfil. This dichotomy – perhaps familiar to some – is played out in the story of Mary and Martha, a story that is often cited as one of the great proof texts for the contemplative tradition of Christian spirituality. 'There is need of only one thing,' says Jesus. 'Mary has chosen the better part, which will not be taken away from her.'[1] In other words, Mary has decided in favour of what really, ultimately, matters. She beholds the truth, manifested before her in the person of Jesus, and it will not be taken away from her because she is anticipating, in her contemplation of Jesus, the eternal contemplation of the soul in communion with God. She is, in this life, living the eternal present moment of the life everlasting.

Martha, on the other hand, is 'worried and distracted by many things'.[2] Martha, like most of us, is caught up in the cares of the world. Martha has to do the things that need doing: she has to work, and get her hands dirty. The story as we have it seems clearly biased in favour of Mary's contemplative calling, appearing to devalue the practical and necessary business

---

1 Luke 10.42
2 Luke 10.41

of everyday life represented by the hard-working Martha. As a consequence many have, not surprisingly, sought to redress the balance. After all, Martha embodies the very real concerns and responsibilities we all face in our daily lives. Most people can probably identify more easily with Martha than Mary, and may well sympathize with the affront she feels on account of the preferential treatment accorded her sister. But maybe that is precisely why Jesus seems to favour Mary, in order to remind us that we need to attend to the often neglected spiritual side of life as well. By affirming the contemplative vocation we are not necessarily devaluing the cares of the world, but making the point that there is more to life than work. Our responsibilities still need our attention, but at the same time we should not allow them to override our spiritual needs altogether; we should keep things in proportion and perspective. There is an appropriate time for everything, as the author of Ecclesiastes sagely observes.[3]

The story of Mary and Martha should not, therefore, be read as a dilemma between two alternative vocations, but rather as an illustration of the need for balance. After all, they are sisters: they share the same DNA. In other words, they do not represent two polar opposites, separate and unrelated, but two sides of the same coin. You cannot have one without the other. In order to be whole, we need both. Indeed, the task of the spiritual life is not to make an 'either–or' choice between the active and contemplative vocations, but to create a 'both–and' synthesis. It is all about balance. Mary and Martha personify two facets of the one calling to pursue what really matters. The question is not which one do we follow, but how do we integrate them? How do we achieve action in contemplation and contemplation in action? How do we, in Paul's words, learn to 'pray without ceasing'?[4] This is not such a difficult concept to grasp. Anyone who has found themselves deeply absorbed in a task – especially one they

---

3 Ecclesiastes 3.1–8
4 1 Thessalonians 5.17

enjoy – or who, like so many of the great saints and mystics, is able to glimpse what is holy in the most mundane activities of life, has experienced contemplation in action. Everything we do should, if possible, be seen as an expression of prayer, and prayer should be seen as a form of work. After all, prayer really is hard work, as anyone who has tried it will no doubt be able to testify.

Most importantly of all, we need to understand from this story that a life of prayer is not just a job for the religious professional. We are all called to seek God, and our own authenticity. Finding the balance between the demands of work – or just everyday life – and our need for spiritual sustenance should be one of our highest priorities: in some way or other it confronts us all. Life can present us with innumerable challenges, including the challenge of finding time for ourselves with energetic young children to look after, the challenge to our faith or values if our work puts us into a compromising situation, or the challenge of remaining positive in the face of illness and infirmity. How, in such circumstances, do we balance Mary and Martha in our lives? How do we balance our necessary concern for the things of this world, our responsibilities to ourselves and one another, with our spiritual calling to seek that which is ultimately real and ultimately true? How do we gain the perspective that will enable and equip us to fulfil our worldly desires and obligations without being deflected from our spiritual aspiration?

Admittedly it is difficult. But, with God, nothing is impossible.[5] Finding this balance – in prayer and in life, in body and in mind – is what meditation, the cultivation of self-awareness through the discipline of stillness, is really all about. The harmony of contemplation in action and action in contemplation is the outward expression of the inner equilibrium we seek to establish by means of our practice. The story of Mary and Martha thus serves as a metaphor for both the spiritual life in general, and also for the specific practice of meditation itself.

---

5 Luke 1.37; Cf. Matthew 19.26